The P scales

The P scales

Assessing the Progress of Children with Special Educational Needs

Written and edited by Francis Ndaji and
Peter Tymms

WILEY-BLACKWELL

A John Wiley & Sons, Ltd., Publication

This edition first published 2009
© 2009 John Wiley & Sons Ltd.

Wiley-Blackwell is an imprint of John Wiley & Sons, formed by the merger of Wiley's global Scientific, Technical, and Medical business with Blackwell Publishing.

Registered Office
John Wiley & Sons Ltd, The Atrium, Southern Gate, Chichester, West Sussex, PO19 8SQ, UK

Editorial Offices
The Atrium, Southern Gate, Chichester, West Sussex, PO19 8SQ, UK
9600 Garsington Road, Oxford, OX4 2DQ, UK
350 Main Street, Malden, MA 02148-5020, USA

For details of our global editorial offices, for customer services, and for information about how to apply for permission to reuse the copyright material in this book please see our website at www.wiley.com/wiley-blackwell.

The right of the editors to be identified as the author of the editorial material in this work has been asserted in accordance with the Copyright, Designs and Patents Act 1988.

Wiley also publishes its books in a variety of electronic formats. Some content that appears in print may not be available in electronic books.

Designations used by companies to distinguish their products are often claimed as trademarks. All brand names and product names used in this book are trade names, service marks, trademarks or registered trademarks of their respective owners. The publisher is not associated with any product or vendor mentioned in this book. This publication is designed to provide accurate and authoritative information in regard to the subject matter covered. It is sold on the understanding that the publisher is not engaged in rendering professional services. If professional advice or other expert assistance is required, the services of a competent professional should be sought.

Library of Congress Cataloging-in-Publication Data

The P scales : assessing the progress of children with special educational needs / written and edited by Francis Ndaji and Peter Tymms.
    p. cm.
    Includes index.
    ISBN 978-0-470-51898-4
  1. Children with disabilities–Education–Great Britain.   2. Educational tests and measurements–Great Britain.   I. Ndaji, Francis.   II. Tymms, Peter.
    LC4036.G7P2 2009
    371.9′043–dc22

                                                                    2009021002

A catalogue record for this book is available from the British Library.

Set in 10.5/13pt Palatino by SNP Best-set Typesetter Ltd., Hong Kong
Printed and bound in Singapore by Fabulous Printers Pte Ltd

1   2009

Contents

About the Authors

Francis Ndaji taught Chemistry and Mathematics in a secondary school, and also worked as a Research Chemist. He joined the Centre for Evaluation and Monitoring (CEM), Durham University in 1999 from Newcastle University where he obtained a PhD in Chemistry and held a research position for four years. Francis is the team leader for the P scales project – the CEM monitoring project for pupils with special educational needs. He is also a member of the Educational Evaluation Group of the Centre.

Peter Tymms After taking a degree in Natural Sciences Peter Tymms taught in a wide variety of schools from Central Africa to the north-east of England before starting an academic career.

He was Lecturer in Performance Indicators at Moray House, Edinburgh before moving to Newcastle University and then to Durham University where he is presently Professor of Education. He is one of the three editors of the *Journal of Early Childhood Research*.

His main research interests include monitoring, assessment, ADHD, reading and research methodology. He devised the PIPS project, which is designed to monitor the affective and cognitive progress of children through primary schools starting with a computer adaptive on-entry baseline assessment. As Director of the CEM, he is responsible for projects monitoring the progress and attitudes of pupils in thousands of schools across the UK and beyond. The CEM is the largest educational research group in a UK university with a staff of 70.

Barbara Riddick is Senior Lecturer in Educational Psychology and Special Needs in the School of Education at Durham University. She researches and teaches in the area of inclusion, diversity and special educational needs. She is also a qualified consultant clinical psychologist with a particular interest in children with severe learning disabilities and autistic spectrum disorders. In the past she has taught children with SENs and in the 1970s was involved in pioneer research looking at the assessment and teaching of children with severe learning disabilities.

Celia Dickinson, Headteacher of a special school since 2002 is one of the first teachers to train in Special Needs Education as a principal subject. She worked extensively with the QCA and DCSF in assessment development especially the P-Levels, and was a member of the writing steering group. Celia has a passion for learning and the way in which people learn. She is a lead learner for Mind-based Learning and a member of the Institute for 21st-Century Learning. She is currently working with The European Agency for Special Needs Education in developing Assessment for Learning based on research into Thinking Skills.

Bob Coburn is the Headteacher of an all-age school for children and students with severe learning difficulties. He holds a PhD in special education and has a passion for working with children who have difficulties in learning and ensuring that they have their entitled access to opportunities to help them live fulfilled lives. Bob also has particular interests in augmentative methods of communication.

Helen Pettinger graduated from Roehampton College of Higher Education in 1997, and after gaining experience in different educational establishments including public and private sector schools, nurseries and pre-school for children with SEN, moved to Mountjoy Special School in 2003. She has worked with pupils across a broad spectrum of difficulty including Down's syndrome, autism, cerebral palsy, etc. and is now leader of a base for children on the autistic spectrum. As part of her role at the school, Helen works in an advisory capacity in a number of mainstream schools, supporting them in their work on inclusion for pupils with special educational needs. Helen assesses children with educational needs using the P scales.

Ginny Brown is the Deputy Headteacher of Montacute School, a school for children who have severe or profound and multiple learning difficulties. She trained at Trent Polytechnic, gaining a BEd in teaching 'mentally handicapped children', was awarded NPQH in 2002 and a Post Graduate Diploma from Plymouth University in 2005. Ginny has spent most of her teaching career working in special schools.

John Parkes has taught within the field of special education for 24 years across the full age and ability range (2–19 years). He holds Bachelors and Masters degrees in Special Education, NPQH and is a member of the Chartered Institute of Educational Assessors. He is presently the Headteacher of Springfield Special School for Pupils with Complex Learning Needs in Knowsley.

Di Brown completed a BEd (Hons) degree in Special Education in 1986. Since then she has worked in three special schools working with pupils with a wide range of special needs. Di was appointed Deputy Headteacher at Springfield School in Crewe in 1998 where she started work with P scales and the Durham Project, to which the school has since contributed annually. In 2004 she completed a research project on the use of P scales in the school for an MA in Education Studies at Manchester Metropolitan University.

Bernie Tetchner began her teaching career in a mainstream primary school in Sydney, Australia. She moved to London and has taught in special schools for 32 years. She has studied at the Institute of Education, London University and has diplomas in SEN, Dyslexia and Autism. Assessment was a major focus of her MA. She is currently Deputy Manager of Lark Hall Centre for pupils with autism in London.

Jo Gilbert has been Headteacher of Manor School in Brent since September 2003. Manor School is a primary special school of 126 pupils with a profile of severe learning difficulties and/or complex learning difficulties. Jo is an active member of the primary and special school's Head Group and serves on a variety of committees, including the Children and Young People Strategic Board and the Schools' Forum.

She was described by an Ofsted inspector as having a motivating and supportive leadership style and an excellent understanding of how the school should improve. She is a SIP to another special school.

Mary Adossides has been Deputy Headteacher of Manor School since September 2003 with main responsibilities for assessment and professional development. She graduated in 1980 and worked in a variety of special schools and colleges in Inner London Education Authority. She is also the designated teacher for child protection. Prior to becoming a Deputy at Manor School, Mary taught across the school from the youngest to the oldest and more complex children. She also taught performing arts and media for three years at the University of Addis Ababa in Ethiopa.

Preface

The time has come for the P scales! Starting 10 years ago, the P scales were created by the Qualifications and Curriculum Authority (QCA) in order to respond to a perceived need to assess children who did not attain at least Level 1 on the National Curriculum. The first attempts at creating the P scales were useful, but there were issues associated with their ability to discriminate between the various areas being assessed. QCA worked with the Centre for Evaluation and Monitoring (CEM) at Durham University to find ways in which the P scales could be improved and how useful feedback to schools could be generated. Over a series of revisions, the P scales got better and better and more widely used. We have now reached the stage where they have become a compulsory feature for all children who do not attain Level 1 on the National Curriculum. It is now vital that good information starts to become available to those people who have to use the P scales for the first time or want to look again at the way in which the system is being implemented. This book is, therefore, very timely and we are sure that it will prove to be very useful.

Francis Ndaji, who wrote the majority of the text, has been working on P scales since we first won the contract with QCA and is an expert on the P scales and all connected matters. The book includes really important inputs from practitioners as well as from Barbara Riddick, a widely published Educational Psychologist. We feel sure that the P scales will continue to evolve. Indeed this is essential as is working with the best possible assessments. We are confident that this volume provides good information that can help the enhancement of the education of all children with special needs in our schools.

Professor Peter Tymms,
Director of the Centre for Evaluation and Monitoring
Durham University

Acknowledgements

We would like to thank Elizabeth Gott, Barbara Hogg and Carole Anderson for reading the manuscript.

We would also like to thank Ucheoma Ndaji for producing the sketches.

CHAPTER 1

The National Curriculum and the Development of the P scales

Francis Ndaji and Peter Tymms

The P scales: Assessing the Progress of Children with Special Educational Needs
Written and edited by Francis Ndaji and Peter Tymms
Copyright © 2009 John Wiley & Sons Ltd.

A Brief History

The Education Reform Act 1988 established the National Curriculum as a nationwide curriculum for all primary and secondary schools in the state school sector in England, Wales and Northern Ireland. It ensured that state schools in all Education Authorities had a common curriculum. On the other hand, Independent Schools were left free to set their own curriculum.

Prior to the publication of the National Curriculum in 1988, the education system was, to a large extent, governed by the Education Act 1944, which had no curriculum requirements with the exception of religious instruction. Until 1988, schools could decide their aims and the curriculum they thought would lead them to those desired aims. This was a potentially problematic situation because schools vary as do teachers and there could be a wide range of differing aims, curricula and standards. Inconsistent standards might lead to:

- schools that did not reflect societal values or the perceived needs of society.
- some pupils leaving school more prepared than others to find jobs and better equipped to adapt to the outside world. Pupils must have the same life chances no matter which school they attended and a National Curriculum should lead to greater equality and to students being able to compete for positions in the job market on an equal footing after they leave school.
- some teachers ill-equipped to deliver curricula that would ensure their pupils could compete fairly with others for jobs on leaving school. Pupils in a school with less sophisticated teachers would be at a disadvantage.

The establishment of the National Curriculum was a recognition that the direction education should take must be determined by the needs and desires of the larger society, and not by teachers at individual schools. Although, initially, many argued against the introduction of the National Curriculum, it was one of those rare initiatives that was later almost universally appreciated. It provided the framework within which schools could develop their own strengths and standards.

The aims of the National Curriculum were:

- the promotion of the spiritual, moral, cultural, mental and physi-cal development of society
- the preparation of pupils for the opportunities, responsibilities and experiences of adult life.

The official position was that in order for it to achieve these aims the National Curriculum must:

- ensure that each pupil, no matter their social background, gender, culture, race, abilities or disabilities, had access to a number of areas of learning to enable them to gain knowledge, understand-ing, skills and the correct attitude required for self-fulfilment and development as responsible members of society.
- make clear to pupils, parents, teachers, governors, employers and the general public the purposes of learning and what learners were expected to gain from their education. It must also set national learning standards based on which the performance of every pupil would be assessed, thereby creating criteria for setting improvement targets and comparison between individual pupils, cohorts of pupils, and schools.
- promote continuity that gives rise to progression in pupil learn-ing. This continuity would make it possible for pupils to move easily from one school to another and to progress from one phase of education to the next. It actually provided a foundation on which lifelong learning profiles would be built.
- enhance the public understanding of the importance and work of schools, and the public appreciation of what schools contribute to the growth of society, in that it provides a common basis on which discussions of educational issues among educational stakeholders could be held.

But society and its needs do not remain static. In order for it to continue to meet the needs for which it was originally established, the National Curriculum has undergone reviews on a regular basis.

The original aims and contents of the National Curriculum were not without criticism. In two separate essays, Professors John White

(2003) and Richard Aldrich (Aldrich and White 1998) of the Institute of Education in London described the National Curriculum, as set out in the Education Reform Act 1988, as being 'excessively brief and thin in substance' and unconnected to the content of the curriculum. In their opinion the relationship between the aims and the 10 subjects of the National Curriculum were not clear. The essays also criticised the fact that the National Curriculum was made compulsory only in the maintained sector, thereby increasing the differentiation between the experiences of children in maintained and independent schools.

In the 1990s pressure started to be exerted to clarify further the purposes of the National Curriculum. The view of teachers, teaching organisations, local authorities and researchers was that the current education system including the National Curriculum was not adequately clear about what it was meant to achieve. This view was not very different from that of the Qualifications and Curriculum Authority (QCA); that the aims and priorities of the school curriculum needed to be better specified. In 2000, a revised National Curriculum was introduced to address the issues with clearer aims and objectives. In a nutshell it stated that:

- the school curriculum should aim to provide opportunities for all pupils to learn and to achieve
- the school curriculum should aim to promote pupils' spiritual, moral, social and cultural development and prepare them for the opportunities, responsibilities and experiences of life.

The details of the amendment, especially the full descriptions of the points above are to be found in the amended document (see also White, 2003).

The importance of education to the individual and society as a whole cannot be over-emphasised. It is the means by which individuals access spiritual, social, cultural and mental development. It should equip them with the ability to respond positively to the challenges of a rapidly changing world and help to establish a commitment to the virtues of truth, justice, honesty, trust and a sense of duty to each other and society.

With these values in mind, the National Curriculum outlines a clear statutory entitlement to learning for all pupils up to the age of 16. It determines what will be taught at every stage of their education and how to assess their performance. The plan is that the curriculum contains the learning items that will enable pupils to acquire the benefits of accessing education. In fact the National Curriculum provides the framework on which schools can devise a curriculum to meet the specific needs of individuals and groups of pupils.

Maintained schools can use the National Curriculum to ensure that pupils receive a balanced and consistent education. Effectively, it lays out the subjects to be taught, the knowledge, skills and understanding required and the standards and attainment targets in each subject. It also sets out how pupils' attainment and progress can be measured. To be effective, a curriculum must aim to give teachers, pupils, parents, employers and the wider community a clear understanding of the skills, knowledge and experience that young people are expected to gain from their education.

Key Stages

The state education system in the UK is divided into Key Stages. Each Key Stage is a broad segment populated by pupils of a given age range. Each Key Stage develops the educational knowledge, understanding and skills that pupils of that age group are expected to achieve by the end of the Key Stage. The Key Stages, the corresponding age groups and the tests that students take at the end of each Key Stage are shown in Table 1.1.

The structure of the National Curriculum is organised by subjects and Key Stages, see Table 1.2. It sets out the targets to be achieved in various subject areas at each Key Stage. Hence each Key Stage has a programme of study setting out what pupils should be taught, and attainment targets indicate the expected standards of pupil performance. Schools are then left to choose how they organise their school curriculum to include the programmes of study which will provide the basis for planning schemes of work.

Many schools develop their curriculum using the National Curriculum as the framework but some schools use the QCA Schemes of Work for help in translating the National Curriculum's objectives into teaching and learning activities.

Table 1.1: Key Stages

Age	Stage	Year	Tests
3–4	Foundation		Foundation Stage Profile
4–5		Reception	
5–6	Key Stage 1	Year 1	
6–7		Year 2	National assessments in English and Mathematics
7–8	Key Stage 2	Year 3	
8–9		Year 4	
9–10		Year 5	
10–11		Year 6	National tests in English, Maths, and Science
11–12	Key Stage 3	Year 7	
12–13		Year 8	
13–14		Year 9	National tests in English, Maths and Science
14–15	Key Stage 4	Year 10	Some children take GCSEs
15–16		Year 11	Most children take GCSEs or other national qualifications

Table 1.2: Key Stages and corresponding school year, pupil age and expected level of attainment in the National Curriculum

Key Stage	School year	Age of pupil	Expected NC level
1	2	7	2
2	6	11	4
3	9	14	5

Subjects of the National Curriculum

The National Curriculum is set out in blocks according to the ages of pupils:

1. Early Learning for 3–5 year olds – the Foundation Stage.
2. The National Curriculum for 5–11 year olds – Key Stages 1 and 2

3. The National Curriculum for 11–16 year olds – Key Stages 3 and 4

The early learning stage for 3–5 year olds

Also known as the Foundation Stage, this is the period from nursery to the end of reception class after which the pupil goes into Year 1 of the primary school. During the Foundation Stage, young children need a well planned and resourced curriculum to take their learning forward and to provide opportunities for all children to succeed in an atmosphere of care and in an environment and with an attitude that gives them the feeling that they are well valued. They follow the Foundation Stage Curriculum, which is organised in six subject areas as shown in the QCA document entitled 'Curriculum guidance for the foundation stage' (QCA 2000). The subject areas are as follows:

- *personal, social and emotional development:* gives children self-confidence, to confer upon them the ability to identify their own needs, to differentiate between right and wrong, and to encourage independence, for example in dressing and undressing themselves.
- *communication, language and literacy:* teaches a child how to speak confidently through participation in activities such as storytelling, singing, speaking and relaying sounds. It also encourages them to attempt to write some words with which they are familiar.
- *mathematical development:* enables a child to understand mathematics through the activities they undertake in the point above, and helps them to familiarise themselves with numbers, shapes and space.
- *knowledge and understanding of the world:* encourages a child to acquire an inquisitive and exploring mind that empowers them to learn about current technologies, different cultures and beliefs.
- *physical development:* teaches a child how to move confidently while controlling their bodies.
- *creative development:* encourages a child to appreciate colours and shapes, to make music and dance, and to acquire and develop particular skills.

The National Curriculum for 5–11 year olds

Children move through Key Stages 1 and 2, where the compulsory National Curriculum subjects are the same for both stages. Of these, English, Mathematics and Science are the 'core subjects' in which pupils take compulsory national tests at the end of Key Stage 2. They study:

- English
- Mathematics
- Science
- Design and Technology
- Information and Communication Technology (ICT)
- History
- Geography
- Art and Design
- Music
- Physical Education.

The National Curriculum for 11–16 year olds

Children move through Key Stages 3 and 4. They take national tests at the end of Key Stage 3 and choose the subjects they will study at Key Stage 4 in preparation for a national qualification, usually GCSEs. They study:

- English
- Mathematics
- Science
- Design and Technology
- Information and Communication Technology (ICT)
- History
- Geography
- Art and Design
- Modern Languages
- Citizenship
- Music
- Physical Education.

Levels of the National Curriculum

The National Curriculum levels are used to describe the results of compulsory assessments of pupils at the end of Years 2, 6 and 9; that is, at ages 7, 11 and 14. Pupils are given levels by their teachers at the end of Year 2 (aged 7) and take national tests at the end of Years 6 and 9. The levels are also used to describe the results of optional tests taken by pupils at Years 3, 4, 5, 7 and 8.

There are eight National Curriculum levels, the highest being Level 8. To derive the levels the range of scores that correspond to each subject level is given to teachers and markers each year. Because they are given each year the scores ranges for the subject levels may vary from one year to another.

There is a level description for each level in each subject. This enables teachers to make a judgement as to which level a pupil has achieved in each subject. The teacher can refer to the National Curriculum levels to make their own assessment of the pupil based on their current work. These assessments are usually fed back to parents at parent–teacher evenings or in the pupil's school report, and they usually indicate at what level of the National Curriculum a child is working in a given subject.

Disapplication of the National Curriculum

Disapplication of the National Curriculum refers to a situation where any part or all of the National Curriculum is not made available to a child because it does not satisfy the child's needs.

The National Curriculum emphasises inclusion and aims at securing learners' participation as well as ensuring that there are appropriate opportunities for them to achieve their potential. However, schools have considerable flexibility within the National Curriculum to develop their own curriculum appropriately to serve the needs of their pupils.

Although the National Curriculum allows headteachers a good degree of flexibility to develop the curriculum in line with the needs of the majority of their pupils, there are cases where the National Curriculum may not maximise the learning and achievement of some pupils. In such cases the full National Curriculum may not be the most appropriate route for the child to pursue learning and achievement and headteachers may in such cases consider disapplying some or all parts of it.

Disapplication may be from all or part of the National Curriculum, all or part of separate programmes of study, or all or part of the statutory assessment arrangements. The advice is that schools should retain pupils' access to a broad and balanced curriculum or learning programme, including as much of the National Curriculum as possible.

There are three conditions under which the National Curriculum can be disapplied:

1. *Temporary disapplication:* This can come about through regulations under Section 93 of the Education Act 2002. Essentially, this section gives permission to headteachers to temporarily discontinue the application of the National Curriculum or parts of it to a pupil or pupils of their school if prevailing conditions do not allow the pupil(s) maximum benefit of the curriculum. The section states that 'regulations may enable the headteacher of a maintained school or maintained nursery school, in such cases or circumstances and subject to such conditions as may be prescribed, to direct in respect of a registered pupil at the school that, for such period as may be specified in the direction (the 'operative period' of the direction), the National Curriculum for England (a) shall not apply, or (b) shall apply with such modifications as may be specified in the direction.'

2. *Statement of Special Educational Needs:* Under Section 92 of the Education Act 2002, a statement of Special Educational Needs could lead to the National Curriculum being disapplied to a child. In essence, this section of the Education Act empowers headteachers to disapply the National Curriculum completely from a child or apply it with necessary modification if that child has been identified as having a Special Educational Need under Section 324 of the Education Act 1996. Disapplication could also be for groups of pupils or the whole school community. The relevant section of the act states that 'the special educational provision for any pupil specified in a statement under Section 324 of the Education Act 1996 (c. 56) of his Special Educational

Needs may include provision (a) excluding the application of the National Curriculum for England, or (b) applying the National Curriculum for England with such modifications as may be specified in the statement.'

3. *To enable curriculum development or experimentation:* Under Section 90 of the Education Act 2002 the National Curriculum can be disapplied for a time-limited period, to enable curriculum development or experimentation. This section of the act states that 'for the purpose of enabling development work or experiments to be carried out, the Secretary of State may direct in respect of a particular maintained school or maintained nursery school that, for such period as may be specified in the direction, the National Curriculum for England (a) shall not apply, or (b) shall apply with such modifications as may be specified in the direction.'

Development of the P scales

The P scales were intended to rationalise the apparent conflict between the National Curriculum and the statement of special educational needs (SENs).

The conflict arose because, while a legal requirement demanded that all children, including those with Special Educational Needs, should access the National Curriculum, it was practically impossible for some because of their Special Educational Needs. It was not until the publication of the P scales that it became possible to determine the attainment and progress of those pupils whose attainments and progress were too low to register in the National Curriculum; that is, below Level 1, of whom many will be found in special schools, though many others will be found in mainstream schools as a result of the increasingly inclusive nature of these schools. Such pupils generally found the National Curriculum too advanced, most of them were classified as having more severe and complex Special Educational Needs.

The P scales are descriptions of attainment levels below Level 1 of the National Curriculum. They describe some of the important knowledge, skills and understanding that pupils may gain from each subject area and were introduced in response to the failure of the National Curriculum assessments to serve the needs of pupils working below Level 1 of the National Curriculum. The scales were first published in 1998 by the DCSF but have since undergone a series of revisions.

Prior to the publication of the P scales, teachers used the code W (working towards Level 1) when the statutory data were collected at the end of the Key Stages, but the code W did not give any information about how far below Level 1 the children were working, neither could it indicate if the children had made any progress over a given period of time. The P scales are now the recommended tool for assessing such pupils.

Other pupils for whom the statutory end of Key Stage tests/tasks were judged to be inappropriate were disapplied from statutory assessments altogether, signified by D. A lot of data were lost this way.

As a result, in the mid 1990s a group of headteachers of special schools came together in order to develop criteria that would be appropriate for measuring the attainment levels and progress of their pupils who had been classified as having Special Educational Needs and for whom the National Curriculum had proved inappropriate. The DfES (as it was then called) became interested in the work the headteachers were doing and the need to develop such criteria and subsequently commissioned the National Foundation for Educational Research (NFER) to develop the criteria further by consultation with special and mainstream staff. Publication of the P scales was the outcome of that consultation.

The development of the P scales enabled teachers to set improvement targets for pupils with Special Educational Needs. They were aimed at summative assessments at the end of Key Stages, although the summative assessments could be conducted at the end of each academic year for those pupils who were making more rapid progress. The P scales did not constitute a curriculum, but were complementary to the National Curriculum in the sense that data collected using the P scales filled the data gap that existed in the national information as a result of the inapplicability of the National Curriculum to the assessment of pupils with Special Educational Needs.

In order for the P scales to apply to any pupil they must have a statement of Special Educational Need. There are many cases where children who have recently arrived in the UK from non-

English speaking countries are achieving below expectations because of their deficiency in the English language. The P scales are not applicable to such pupils.

The first version of the P scales published in 1998 covered three subject areas, namely, English, Mathematics and Personal and Social Development (PSD). These subject areas were further split into strands as follows:

English

- Reading
- Writing
- Speaking and listening.

Mathematics

- Using and applying
- Number
- Shape, space and measures.

Personal and Social Development (PSD)

- Interacting and working with others
- Independent and organisation skills
- Attention.

The attainment levels in the English strands of the first version of the assessment criteria were from P1 to P8 and extended to the National Curriculum Levels 1–3. Levels 1 and 2 of the National Curriculum were each subdivided into three such that Level 1 comprised 1A, 1B and 1C, and Level 2 comprised 2A, 2B and 2C.

Each of the Mathematics strands had P scales attainment levels of P1–P8 while each of the three strands of PSD had attainment levels of 1–15.

A major review of the P scales took place in 2001 leading to the publication of a booklet titled *Supporting the target setting process – Guidance for effective target setting for pupils with special educational needs*. The booklet contained P scales assessment criteria for the core subjects, namely, English, Mathematics and Science. Subsequently P scales were published for all National Curriculum subjects (QCA

2001). The review of the P scales in 2001 split each of the levels P1, P2 and P3 into two sub levels. P1 was split into P1(i) and P1(ii), P2 into P2(i) and P2(ii), and P3 into P3(i) and P3(ii). Levels P1(i) to P3(ii) in each subject indicated the earliest levels of general attainment and were common to all subjects. The splitting of P1 to P3 of the P scales into sub-levels was in response to a report by teachers who had found that some of their pupils, especially those who had very serious Special Educational Needs such as Profound and Multiple Learning Difficulty (PMLD), found it very difficult to progress through even the very lowest levels of the P scales. The aim of splitting P1, P2 and P3 of the P scales into sub-levels was to increase the sensitivity of the scales at these very low levels of attainment.

The science subject area had four strands:

- Scientific enquiry
- Life processes and living things
- Materials and their properties
- Physical properties.

P1(i) to P8 were generic to all four strands of Science, unlike English and Mathematics where only P1(i) to P3(ii) were generic to all strands. Thus P1(i) to P3(ii) applied to all strands of English and Mathematics while P4 to L2A were subject-specific descriptions of each attainment level from P4 to L2A. Likewise, P1(i) to P8 applied to all strands of Science while Levels 1 and 2 were subject-specific descriptions of attainment levels (see Table 1.3).

In the 2001 review, PSD (Personal and Social Development) was replaced with PSHE (Personal Social and Health Education). While PSD had three strands and 15 levels of attainment in each strand, PSHE had only one strand of 8 attainment levels.

The review also produced P scales criteria published in separate booklets for the following subjects:

- Modern Foreign Languages
- Geography
- History
- Developing Skills
- Art and Design

Table 1.3: Generic levels of the cognitive scales (2001 version)

	English				Mathematics			Science			
	Speaking	Listening	Reading	Writing	Using and applying	Number	Shape, space and measures	Scientific enquiry	Life processes and living things	Materials and their properties	Physical properties
Generic levels	P1(i), P1(ii), P2(i), P2(ii), P3(i), P3(ii)							P1(i), P1(ii), P2(i), P2(ii), P3(i), P3(ii), P4, P5, P6, P7, P8			

- Music
- Design Technology
- Information and Communications Technology (ICT)
- Religious Education
- Physical Education.

In 2004 a further review of the P scales was carried out resulting in:

- the creation of separate strands for Speaking and Listening from a combined measure
- the review of attainment level descriptions between P4 and Level 1 in response to the request of practitioners
- the creation of a combined Speaking and Listening strand for pupils who achieve above P8 in the Speaking and the Listening strands of English.

Following this review Speaking and Listening strands have attainment levels in the range of P1(i) to P8. At levels 1 and higher they are combined under the heading Speaking and listening. The creation of a combined Speaking and listening strand (for NC level scores) in addition to the separate strands of Speaking and Listening resulted in a lot of confusion for teachers during data collection and recording. The problems arising from this will be discussed in a later chapter.

Introduction of the P scales into Schools

In 1999 the QCA appointed the Centre for Evaluation and Monitoring (CEM) at Durham University to conduct a data collection exercise. The aims of the data collection were:

- to present a national picture of the performances of pupils who work below age-related expectations; that is pupils who work below Level 1 of the National Curriculum
- to analyse the data and prepare feedback for schools so that they could use it for self-evaluation and for setting improvement targets for their pupils.

The Centre for Evaluation and Monitoring (CEM) at Durham University conducted the data collection exercise annually from 1999 to 2004 on behalf of the QCA. The participation of schools in the data collection exercise was voluntary. The starting number of schools was 295 and by 2004, the last year the exercise was conducted on behalf of the QCA, the number of schools had risen to 1029. Similarly, the number of pupils in the data collection rose annually from 12,554 in 1999 to 30,029 in 2004. The numbers are shown in Figures 1.1 and 1.2 respectively.

Since 2005 the CEM has conducted the data collection exercise not on behalf of the QCA but as a CEM project, paid for by the schools. This project has involved about 500 schools. In the summer of 2005, the DfES (now the DCSF) invited schools to report as a P level the attainment levels of any child having Special Educational Need and working below level 1 of the National Curriculum. This invitation was one of the first steps towards making mandatory the use of P scales and the collection and submission of P scales data by schools starting from the summer of 2007 – a change that would make the P scales part of the National Curriculum. Although Section 87 of the Education Act 2002 empowered the Secretary of State to

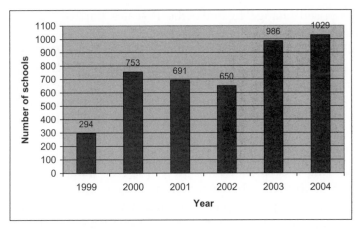

Figure 1.1: Number of schools in the P scales data collection project each year from 1999 to 2004.

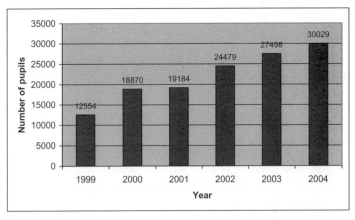

Figure 1.2: Numbers of pupils in the P scales data collection project from 1999 to 2004.

revise the National Curriculum for England for the Foundation Stage and the Key Stages whenever they considered revision necessary or expedient, the Secretary of State was required to issue the appropriate orders and regulations under that section in order to carry out the changes. Therefore, from 7 September to 29 November 2006 the QCA consulted, on behalf of the Secretary of State, on the proposed change to make the P scales part of the National Curriculum.

Following a satisfactory consultation by QCA, the P scales (originally planned for summer 2007) became part of the National Curriculum from September 2008 and the recording of pupils' achievement and progress using the P scales became statutory. From 2008, schools will be required to report the attainments of pupils with Special Educational Needs who are working below Level 1 of the National Curriculum at the end of Key Stages 1, 2 and 3. This means that relevant pupil Key Stage data will be collected with their achievement and progress from 2008. P scales will be used to report pupils' attainments and progress in National Curriculum core subjects at the end of Key Stages 1 and 2, and on core and foundation subjects at the end of Key Stage 3.

Uses of the P scales in Schools

The P scales were established to provide schools with an appropriate system with which to assess the attainment of pupils who have Special Educational Needs, but to what use can schools put the attainment data?

Summative assessment

The P scales can be used for summative assessment of pupils. Such summative data might be useful in reporting to parents or as general information for the school.

Target setting

The data can be used in setting improvement targets. The average attainment in a chosen subject for pupils with the same principal educational need but a year group higher should be the starting point in the process of setting a target for a pupil in that subject. This assumes that the older year group has made an average attainment that is higher than the pupil's attainment. The current attainment level of the pupil must also be taken into consideration so that the target is neither too high nor too low.

Identification of pupil skills

The data can be used in identifying the subject areas in which a pupil is doing better than in others. It could also identify a pupil's skills.

Identification of progress

The attainment data can be used in tracking a pupil's year on year attainment in each subject. The information can be used in identifying the subject areas in which the pupil makes more progress and in establishing a pattern of progress.

Identification of general patterns in the school's data

The aggregation of data by cohorts of pupils enables the P scales data to be used in examining the overall school performance in all subjects and by cohorts, such as special need categories and year groups. For example, the average pupil performance in each subject could be calculated and a comparison made between the school average score in each subject. Also the average score of each year group for each special need could be calculated and compared.

Feeding back to parents and guardians/carers

Parents and carers evenings afford parents and carers the opportunity to discuss pupils' achievements. Prior to the publication of the P scales teachers of pupils working below Level 1 of the National Curriculum had no official means of showing parents/carers the attainment or progress that their children had made. The P scales give parents and guardians the chance to celebrate the progress of their children who are working below Level 1.

Comparison of data with other schools

Schools may want to compare their pupils' attainment data with those of other schools. The P scales give them the opportunity to do so, but they should take care to compare like with like. They should be able to compare the average attainments of a particular category of special need and year group with those of a similar cohort in other schools.

Special Need Groups

According to Section 312 of the Education Act 1996 a child has Special Educational Needs if: 'he [sic] has a learning difficulty that calls for a special educational provision to be made for him.'

A child could also be defined as having a learning difficulty if:

- the child has a significantly greater difficulty in learning than the majority of children of their age, or
- the child has a disability which either prevents or hinders them from making use of educational facilities of a kind generally provided for children of their age in schools within the area of the local education authority.

The same Act states that 'a child is not to be taken as having a learning difficulty solely because the language (or form of the language) in which he [sic] is, or will be, taught is different from a language (or form of a language) which has at any time been spoken in his [sic] home.' This is very relevant to pupils who have arrived in the U.K. from non-English speaking countries to whom English is a second language. In order that such pupils are classified as having a learning difficulty it must be established that learning difficulty is the only reason for which they perform below expectations. The DCSF advised teachers to record as W the attainments for children who are learning English as a second language and working below Level 1 of the National Curriculum.

Categories of Special Educational Needs

There are several types of educational need but they can be placed in four main categories which can then be subdivided.

1. Cognition and learning needs
   - Specific Learning Difficulty (SpLD)
   - Moderate Learning Difficulty (MLD)
   - Severe Learning Difficulty (SLD)
   - Profound and Multiple Learning Difficulty (PMLD)
2. Behavioural, emotional and social development needs
   - Behavioural, Emotional and Social Difficulty (BESD)

3. Communication and interaction needs
   • Speech, Language and Communication Needs (SLCN)
   • Autistic Spectrum Disorder (ASD)
4. Sensory and/or physical needs
   • Visual Impairment (VI)
   • Hearing Impairment (HI)
   • Multi-Sensory Impairment (MSI)
   • Physical Disability (PD)

A fifth category named 'Other' only applies to pupils at School Action Plus where the educational need is not clearly identified.

Children are not to be recorded as having a Special Educational Need unless a statement of Special Educational Need (SEN) has been obtained for them. The category 'Other' must not be used if a child already has a statement of SEN. The procedure for obtaining a statement of Special Educational Need is described in the SEN Code of Practice on the DCSF website at http://www.dfes. gov.uk/publications/guidanceonthelaw/dfeepub/jul00/020700/ index.htm

Pupils who have English as their second language or have medical conditions must not be categorized as having Special Educational Need unless a statement identifying a Special Educational Need has been obtained for them. In cases where more than one Special Educational Need is recognised the most serious need is identified as the primary need.

Use of the P scales in Mainstream Schools

Although special schools were established for pupils with learning difficulties and other disabilities, a large number of pupils with statements of Special Educational Need are in state-maintained mainstream schools. In fact DCSF figures show that about 75% of pupils with statements of SEN are placed in mainstream schools. This figure has been increasing since the Special Education and Disability Act 2001, which required LEAs to place children with SEN in mainstream schools unless it is incompatible with the choice of their parents or with the provision of efficient education for other children, for example where a pupil presents a challenging behaviour that significantly disrupts other pupils' learning. This policy is known as 'inclusion' and it aims to ensure that pupils with Special Educational Needs and other disabilities can learn, play and live together with other pupils in pre-school provision, schools, colleges, etc., with the appropriate support. Inclusion enables pupils with statements of Special Educational Need to participate in the normal activities of mainstream schools to the best of their abilities.

Because they are expected to play a role in society in their adult lives, pupils with Special Educational Needs should, like other pupils, be prepared properly for such roles, and an early start in mainstream nursery schools and, later, admission to mainstream schools and colleges is seen as essential.

With so many pupils with statements of SEN in mainstream schools it was expected that the P scales would be widely used in mainstream schools. This does not seem to have been the case. The participation information in the P scales data collection project at Durham University sponsored by the DCSF/QCA from 1999 to 2004 is shown in Table 1.4.

As explained previously, the P scales data collection and analysis project from which Table 1.4 was derived was financially supported by the QCA from 1999 to 2004. It was expected that all schools or at least a large majority of schools that used the P scales would participate as they did not have to pay participation fees. However, it can be seen from Table 1.4 that more than 75% of pupils who were enrolled in the project each year came from special schools. Similarly, it was expected that a larger percentage of the pupils

Table 1.4: Percentage distribution of special and mainstream schools in the P scales project from 1999 to 2004

Year	Pupils from mainstream schools (%)	Pupils from special schools (%)
1999	16.3	83.7
2000	24.3	75.7
2001	19.7	80.3
2002	15.9	84.1
2003	17.9	82.1
2004	19.6	80.4

would come from mainstream schools in view of the government's inclusion policy that required most pupils to be taught in mainstream schools irrespective of whether or not they have Special Educational Needs. However, it was possible that most pupils with SEN in mainstream schools were working above the P scales.

References

Aldrich R and White J (1998) The National Curriculum Beyond 2000: The QCA and the Aims of Education. London: Institute of Education, University of London. DfEE (2001) *Supporting the target setting process – Guidance for effective target setting for pupils with special educational needs*. London: DfEE.

QCA (2000) Curriculum guidance for the foundation stage, QCA/00/587, http://www.direct.gov.uk

QCA (2001) *Planning, teaching and assessing the curriculum for pupils with learning difficulties*. London: QCA. www.qca.org.uk/ld/index.html

White J (2003) Rethinking the School Curriculum: Values, Aims, and Purposes. London: Routledge Falmer.

Further Reading

Education Act 2003, Section 93.

www.dfes.gov.uk/publications/guidanceonthelaw/dfeepub/jul00/020700/index.htm

www.direct.gov.uk/en/EducationAndLearning/Schools/ExamsTestsAndTheCurriculum/DG_4016665www.nc.uk.net/nc_resources/html/inclusion.shtml

www.parentscentre.gov.uk/educationandlearning/whatchildrenlearn/curriculumandassessment/thenationalcurriculum/

www.teachernet.gov.uk.

CHAPTER 2

P scales – The Context

Barbara Riddick

The P scales: Assessing the Progress of Children with Special Educational Needs
Written and edited by Francis Ndaji and Peter Tymms
Copyright © 2009 John Wiley & Sons Ltd.

In 1971 an important event took place, the 1970 Education Act came into force. This stipulated for the first time that all children were 'educable'. Until this point some 24,000 children in special care units and junior training centres plus another 8,000 in 'sub-normality' hospitals had been deemed as uneducable and, although they were entitled to care, they were not entitled to an education because it was argued they were incapable of learning. Accompanying the 1970 act, pioneering research projects at Queen Mary's Hospital in Carshalton and at the Hornsey Centre in London, set out to demonstrate that, with the appropriate structured teaching, children formerly seen as uneducable could learn and progress (Kiernan and Riddick 1973; Riddick and Kiernan 1972). It was obvious to everybody involved in the Queen Mary project that most of the children were progressing, with many learning self-help, social and play skills for the first time, but they were classified as having severe or profound learning difficulties with IQ scores of less than 50 on the Binet or Weschler Intelligence Scales.

At the time there were no valid comprehensive standardised scales that could be used to evaluate the progress made by such children and some of these project children were recorded as untestable by the hospital's clinical psychologists because they were not able to sit down and co-operate with the tester and could not comprehend or follow verbal instructions. The author vividly remembers the clinical psychologist coming to assess one of the livelier project children on a warm summer day. Within a few minutes the small green wooden blocks from the Binet Intelligence Test were sailing out of the open window and the sound of the untestable stamp could be heard thumping onto the report form. Although this sounds mildly amusing, it underlines the serious lack of attention and thought that was being given to assessing children with severe and complex learning needs. One of the major challenges these projects faced was finding valid ways of assessing and documenting the children's learning progress.

As well as the usual challenges that all assessments face, it can be argued that there are additional challenges involved in designing assessments for children with severe and complex needs, many of whom have accompanying sensory or motor difficulties, raising questions about how to design assessment that is accessible, for example, to a child who is blind or cannot control their hand and arm movements. Should items that would disadvantage them be excluded, should an alternative but equivalent item be designed, or should a way of helping them access the item be found? A significant proportion of such children will be nonverbal and some will have little, if any, speech comprehension, requiring alternative ways of assessing progress without the use of verbal or written responses. A final issue is how to ensure that children understand what is required of them and are sufficiently motivated to engage in the assessment process.

Prevalence and Categorisation of Disabilities/SENs

'Prevalence' refers to the total number of individuals with a particular disability/SEN within a given population and is usually expressed as a percentage. For example, the BDA (British Dyslexia Association) estimates that roughly 4% of school children have moderate to severe dyslexia.

'Incidence' refers to the number of new instances of a disability within a given time frame (usually a year). Some disabilities such as visual impairments are termed 'low incidence' conditions because of the relatively small numbers occurring in the school population.

In the USA, for a number of years, the federal government has issued an annual report on the number of individuals with disabilities/SENs (Annual Report to Congress under the Individuals with Disabilities in Education Act). Obviously these figures are only as good as the accuracy of the categories into which the children are placed. Because of concerns over this, the UK government did not collect figures for several years in the 1990s and early 2000s, but in its report *Removing Barriers to Achievement* (DfES 2004) it said that the collection of figures would be reinstated. This was part of a long running debate within SEN on how children with disabilities/SENs should be identified and categorised. Some of the arguments and misgivings over categorisation date back to the Warnock Report (DES 1978) and have been well rehearsed. They include:

- The use of medical categories such as cerebral palsy or Down's syndrome, which do not indicate the very variable learning needs of children within these categories.
- The danger of seeing SENs as fixed and unchangeable, whereas a child might be deemed to have SEBDs (Social, Emotional and Behavioural Difficulties) in one setting or stage of development but not in another.
- The danger of seeing children with SENs as a distinctly separate group from other children rather than as part of a continuum of difference and diversity.

Pre the Warnock Report, 10 statutory categories of handicap dating back to the Education Act 1944 were in use:

1. Pupils who were blind
2. Pupils who were deaf
3. Pupils who had partial sight
4. Pupils who had partial hearing
5. Pupils who were delicate
6. Pupils who had speech defects
7. Pupils who were maladjusted
8. Pupils who had epilepsy
9. Pupils who were educationally subnormal
10. Pupils who had physical handicap.

The Warnock Report (DES 1978) recommended the abolition of the statutory categories of handicap. It proposed that, at any time, approximately 20% of school-age children were likely to have a Special Educational Need, which should be seen as a continuum of need shading into the ordinary everyday needs of the classroom. The report distinguished between the 18% of children who had relatively mild or transient difficulties and the 2% of children who had more severe, complex and long lasting difficulties. It was suggested that the needs of the 18% should be met within the schools' existing framework whereas the 2% would require additional specialised provision. In order to protect the needs of the 2% of children with more severe difficulties, Statements of Special Educational Needs were introduced by the Education Act 1981, which translated the recommendations of the Warnock Report into legislation. The

Warnock Report also recommended that more children with SENs should be integrated into mainstream school and that parents should be consulted and involved in their children's assessment and education. As a consequence of this legislation, Special Educational Need (SEN) was introduced as a legally defined term.

Whilst much of this is history, some important threads of continuity and controversy run through into current SEN policy. The return to collecting annual figures on the numbers of children in different categories of SEN indicates the continuing dilemma about the best way to characterise and help them. Despite the problems of discrete categories the figures do give some indication, for example, of the number of children with hearing impairments who need to be catered for in a given school year.

In the Revised SEN Code of Practice (DfES 2001), four main areas of educational difficulty or need were suggested with a back up category of 'other' for any difficulties or needs not captured by the four.

1. Cognition and Learning Difficulties
2. Behavioural, Emotional and Social Development Needs
3. Communication and Interaction Needs
4. Sensory and/or Physical Needs
5. Other (OTH)

The Code of Practice did acknowledge that these were not 'hard and fast categories of special educational need' (p 85) and that some children may have needs that fall into two or three of these categories. A useful function of the definition of these four areas of need is that they underline the fact that educational difficulties can arise because of fundamental cognitive, affective, social or physical/ sensory difficulties. These are, to a lesser or greater degree, dependent on environmental circumstances, and a primary difficulty in one area can sometimes lead to secondary difficulties in another. One enduring debate is what level of specificity any categorisation of Special Educational Needs should adopt. As soon as the above categories are examined in any detail, it is clear that individual children within a single designated area of need may have very different educational requirements. A child with a specific learning difficulty such as dyslexia will have very different learning needs from a child with profound and complex learning difficulties, although they both come under the area of cognition and learning difficulties. It is thus unsurprising to find that, as soon as these four areas of need were applied to school settings by Ofsted, relatively specific sub areas of need were identified within each category.

These categories have been sub-divided by Ofsted into:

1. Cognition and Learning Difficulties
   - Specific Learning Difficulties (SpLD) e.g. dyslexia,
   - Moderate Learning Difficulties (MLD)
   - Severe Learning Difficulty (SLD)
   - Profound and Multiple Learning Difficulty (PMLD)
2. Behaviour, Emotional and Social Development Needs
   - Behaviour, Emotional and Social Difficulties (BESD)
3. Communication and Interaction Needs
   - Speech, Language and Communication Needs (SLCN)
   - Autistic Spectrum Disorders (ASD)
4. Sensory and/or Physical Needs
   - Visual Impairment (VI)
   - Hearing Impairment (HI)
   - Multi-Sensory Impairment (MSI)
   - Physical Disability
5. Other (OTH)

It is interesting to compare these contemporary categories of need with the pre-Warnock (1978) categories of educational need. It can be seen that five of the pre-Warnock categories would fall into the current category of physical and sensory needs, pupils with 'educational sub-normality' would now appear in the category of 'learning difficulties', and 'maladjusted pupils' would now fall in the category of 'pupils with social, behavioural and emotional difficulties'. Likewise, pupils who had speech defects would now be in the category of 'communication difficulties'. Pupils who had epilepsy or were deemed delicate in the pre-Warnock categories do not map directly onto existing categories. A criticism that Warnock made was that medical categories such as epilepsy did not accurately indicate educational need and should therefore be abandoned as an educational category. Children with epilepsy would now only feature indirectly in SEN categories if their epilepsy led to specific difficulties in learning or behaviour. Some categories such as autistic spectrum disorders or specific learning difficulties were not recognised officially pre-Warnock and indicate the changing landscape of Special Educational Needs. From a historical perspective categories of SENs change in prominence for social, psychological and medical reasons and will probably continue to do so. Despite these changes it is instructive to see how many categories of SEN have endured over time in one form or another. Some might see this as a failure of current educational policy to break away from past thinking, but it could prompt us to consider both positive and negative aspects of categorisation. Perhaps the most important shift has been in how categories are used, with the emphasis now on the individual first and then the category. So we talk about a person with a hearing impairment or a learning disability rather than a hearing impaired or learning disabled person. Norwich (2007) discussed what he called 'dilemmas of difference' (p 61) in that there are both advantages and disadvantages to categorising children with SENs. He proposed that one way forward is to place specific group based needs within the wider context of the common educational needs of all children. He suggested the following three-dimensional model:

1. general needs common to all
2. specific needs common to group membership
3. unique needs.

To date, most attention has been on the specific categories used and there has been relatively little research into how people apply and respond to particular categories. What may be important is how subtly and constructively categories are used and whether their ultimate purpose is to enable and support children's learning and general wellbeing. An EU Report (Meijer et al. 2003) on SENs noted that countries varied in the number of categories they used from two in Denmark to an average of 6–10 across most European countries. As the report points out, these do not reflect actual variations in the number or type of SENs in different countries, just differences in ideology, policy and funding. A more fundamental question would be how effectively the learning needs of children with SENs are met across different countries. It is interesting to note that neither the EU report nor the more recent Commons report in the UK pay real attention to the issue of how the learning of children with SENs is assessed and monitored.

Schools using the P scales have commented that comparing the progress of children across schools within a broad category such as severe learning difficulty is not appropriate (Byers 2003). Children with severe learning difficulties vary so much in terms of their individual learning profiles that it is almost impossible to make a meaningful comparison between them in terms of progress. It is also the case that a child at KS1 who is scoring at P2 on the P scales is very different from a child at KS3 or KS4 who is still scoring at P2 on the P scales. For this reason Byers recommends reporting children's progress relative to their past performance, their current attainment and their chronological age.

Models of SEN

Perhaps as important as the categorisation of SENs are the attributions or explanations that are given for any particular child's SENs; that is, the particular model of SEN that is applied. At one extreme these have been characterised as child or individual psychological factors, at the other, environmental or social factors.

An environmental perspective

This argues that we should be looking at how the environment influences learning rather than at individual differences. It could be seen as an understandable reaction to previous over reliance on 'within child' explanations of difficulty. In an extreme form this postulates that there is no such thing as a learning disability, only inappropriate learning environments that do not teach children in such a way that they learn. Ainscow (2007) has consistently argued that meeting special needs should be integrated into the overall design and delivery of the whole school curriculum rather than be seen as something separate and additional.

Some claim that the main cause of learning problems is that the curriculum moves too fast and doesn't start with the skills a child has, therefore placing impossible demands on them (Solity 1996).

This has parallels with the social model of disability perspective which argues that people are not disabled, it is the environments they have to live in that disable them.

There is some evidence in support of the environmental perspective. Some schools are more successful than others in supporting children in their learning and some schools appear to 'produce' more children with special needs (Rutter et al. 1979). This applies particularly to children with mild-to-moderate learning difficulties or social, emotional and behavioural difficulties. It could be argued that this environmental awareness has been helpful in focusing on whole school issues and how learning is organised and delivered for all children.

Individual differences sometimes called a 'within child' model

Wearmouth (2000) posits a counter argument that, in some aspects, not to acknowledge difference can be counterproductive to the learning needs of some students and disrespectful of their life experiences. Frederickson and Cline (2002) argue that it is important to know and understand about the individual differences children bring to their learning as this can help inform the best way to teach them. For example, a considerable body of research has demonstrated that children with autism learn more effectively through visual as opposed to auditory methods. This has led to successful approaches like TEACH that have incorporated this information in their teaching methods.

Dockrell and McShane (1993) reported over a series of studies that when children with Down's syndrome were compared with other children with the same degree of learning disability they found distinct differences in their learning profiles. Down's syndrome children were slower in organising their motor responses and therefore needed more time and practise in speaking or responding to questions or carrying out tasks. Allowing more time or giving them more practice at motor skills considerably enhanced their overall performance.

An interactional perspective

Tomlinson (1982) suggested that 'neither fatalistic psychological views of individual causality nor simple sociological views of environmental determinism should go unchallenged'. Gutierrez and Stone (1997) argued that due attention should be given to both environmental and individual variables.

An interactional analysis views the level of need as the result of a complex interaction between the child's strengths and weaknesses, and assesses the level of support available and the appropriateness of the education being provided. There is currently widespread support for this view and for the view that neither individually nor environmentally focused conceptualisations are adequate on their own (Frederickson and Cline 2002, p 42).

As Frederickson and Cline suggested, there was strong support for an interactional perspective or model of SENs that paid due attention to both individual and environmental factors in understanding a particular child's Special Educational Needs. In reality the issue is often about the degree of emphasis given to these two perspectives and there can still be disagreement and lack of consensus between practitioners both in the same profession and across professions. These models of SEN may sound somewhat removed from classroom practice but they do have an important bearing on how educationalists perceive and respond to children's difficulties.

The Background to Current SEN Policy

Following on from the Warnock report in 1978, which advocated the integration of more children with SENs into mainstream schools, there has been a stream of global and UK reports recommending their inclusion. Commentators argued that, whereas integration was primarily about individual children with SENs fitting into mainstream school, the term inclusion was supposed to denote the systemic changes schools would make in order to adapt to the needs of the child.

In 1997 the new Labour government published a green paper entitled *Excellence for all Children* (DfES 1997) in which they aligned themselves with the global push for the inclusion of as many children as possible in mainstream school. This could be seen as part of a wider concern about issues of diversity, social justice and inclusion in society in general. In 1994, the SEN Code of Practice was published and, in the light of experience, a Revised SEN Code of Practice was issued in 2001 (DfES 2001). The DfES stipulated that

LEAs, schools and other agencies helping them such as the health service must have regard to it. This was also influenced by the new statutory duties required of schools and LEAs by the Special Educational Needs and Disability Act 2001. This required that from 2002 schools must not treat a child less favourably because of their disability and should make reasonable adjustments to ensure they are not placed at a disadvantage. The Code of Practice defined a child as having a Special Educational Need if they required greater help in learning than their peers of the same age or had a disability that prevented them from accessing the learning environment in the usual way.

The Revised Code of Practice tried to lessen some of the bureaucratic burden of the original Code of Practice by reducing the number of recorded levels of intervention for children with SENs to two, School Action and School Action Plus. At the School Action level additional support was to be devised by class teachers in collaboration with the school's SENCO (Special Educational Needs Co-ordinator). For children who did not make progress with this level of support, professionals from outside the school could be called on for additional assessment, support and specialist interventions, in other words School Action Plus. The Revised Code of Practice emphasised the need to involve children in their own assessment and support as far as possible and to pay attention to their wishes. Similarly, the importance of working in partnership with parents was also stressed, with parents ideally having key input in both the assessment process and the proposed plan of intervention.

The Code of Practice went on to state that plans of support and intervention for specific children should be recorded in the form of an Individual Education Plan (IEP) and that this should be reviewed twice a year. The plan was to include specific achievable targets with specified criteria of success, the teaching strategies to be used and the provision put in place. If, despite appropriate plans being put into action, the child still did not progress or progressed very slowly, then, after a process of statutory assessment, the child would be issued with a Statement of Special Educational Needs. This set out a child's precise learning needs and the educational provision required to meet those needs including staffing, equipment and any National Curriculum modifications or exemptions.

Table 2.1: DfES (now DCSF) annual figures on the number and percentage of children with statements of SEN

ALL SCHOOLS	2003	2004	2005	2006	2007
Pupils with statements	250,550	247,590	242,580	236,750	229,110
Pupils on roll	8,366,780	8,334,880	8,274,470	8,215,690	8,149,180
Incidence (%)	3.0	3.0	2.9	2.9	2.8

In January 2007 it was reported that 2.8% of pupils in school in England (229,110) had Statements of SEN, a slight decrease from the previous year when 2.9% of pupils in school were reported to have Statements. Of these statemented children 57% were in mainstream schools, 37% were in maintained special schools and 4% were in independent schools (2% were 'other'). In addition, there was a much larger group of pupils with SENs without Statements who made up 16.4% of pupils across all schools.

SEN Policy and the National Curriculum

An important factor interacting with SEN policy was the launch of the National Curriculum in 1988 (revised 2000), accompanied by regular testing of all children in order to produce national league tables of schools' performance. It was a legal requirement that all children follow the National Curriculum including those with SENs, although limited use could be made of disapplications from parts of the curriculum for individual children. This, it could be argued, had both positive and negative consequences for the education of children with SENs.

On the positive side children with SENs should have access to the same breadth of learning experiences as all children, irrespective of whether they were in a mainstream school, a special school or a special unit. The National Curriculum should also facilitate the movement of both teachers and children between special and mainstream schools and underline that children with SENs are an integral part of the wider school body and not a separate and discrete entity. It might raise the expectations and quality of teaching in relation to SEN across school settings.

On the negative side there were concerns that the academic focus of the National Curriculum was not appropriate for many children with more severe and complex special needs. Some special schools had developed innovative and specialised curriculums focused on the particular learning needs of their children (Ware 2005). Many placed a strong emphasis on independence, self-help and social skills. For children with severe and profound learning difficulties, there was an additional focus on sensory, motor and play skills and the development of responsive environments to facilitate autonomy, communication and social interaction. Teaching often included specific coaching in skills taken for granted in ordinary children, such as learning to visually track an object or learning about object permanence (objects that fall out of view still exist). Even basic skills like these can, in some cases, take a term's work to teach, and will need breaking down into a number of steps. In 2007 just over 30,000 pupils were categorised as having Severe Learning Difficulties with another 8,670 categorised as having Profound and Multiple Learning Difficulties (DfES 2007). The DCSF (2007) suggested that children in these two categories were the ones most likely to be assessed using P scales.

Current SEN Policy

In a European Report on Special Educational Needs, Meijer, Soriano and Watkins (2003) noted that most European countries had policies that were moving towards the greater inclusion of children with SENs in mainstream schools with levels of training, resources and additional teaching assistance varying between countries.

The report proposed that European countries could be loosely divided into three categories in terms of their policy on the inclusion of children with SENs into mainstream schools.

The 'one-track' approach was characterised by the inclusion of nearly all children into mainstream school with attendant support and services delivered within this setting. The countries reported to have adopted this approach were Spain, Greece, Italy, Portugal, Sweden, Iceland, Norway and Cyprus.

The 'multi-tracked' approach to inclusion offered a diverse range of services in mainstream and special school settings. Countries listed under this approach included the United Kingdom along with Denmark, France, Ireland, Luxembourg, Austria, Finland, Latvia, Liechtenstein, the Czech Republic, Estonia, Lithuania, Poland, Slovakia and Slovenia.

The third approach was termed the 'two-tracked' approach because there was distinctly separate educational provision for children with SENs either in special classes or schools. Switzerland, Germany and Belgium fell into this category, but it was acknowledged that the situation was changing with more support being developed in mainstream schools.

At the moment it is open to debate whether the UK plans to move towards a one-track system or to maintain its multi-track system. In 2004 the government published their strategy for SEN under the title of *Removing Barriers to Achievement* (DfES 2004). In this they stated that 'we are firmly committed to the principle of inclusion and an increasing proportion of children with SEN attend mainstream schools' (executive summary, p12). Despite the prominence of this statement at the beginning of Chapter 2 supporting the inclusion of children into mainstream schools under 'what we want', we find 'special schools providing education for children with the most severe and complex needs'. The SEN strategy could be seen as an attempt to marry the ideals of inclusion with some of the realities of service delivery, but the government has been accused of sitting on the fence. Proponents of full inclusion were disappointed and critical of the government for not making a firm commitment to full inclusion with the abolition of all special schools. Critics of full inclusion were equally concerned that the government was pressing ahead with further inclusion despite the reservations of a substantial number of parents of children with Special Educational Needs as well as educationalists.

A recent House of Commons report (Education and Skills Committee 2006) has criticised the government for giving unclear and confusing messages about their long-term goals in relation to inclusion. The Commons Report notes that Lord Adonis, the Minister responsible for SENs, says the government does not have a set view on how many children should attend special schools and they would be 'content' to let the current status quo prevail. At present approximately 1% of children attend special schools and, without explicitly saying so, the government seem to be agreeing that this is an appropriate figure. The Commons Report urges the government to be 'upfront' about its inclusion policy and to be clear about whether they are signalling a change in direction. This is an important issue for both special and mainstream schools.

Special schools have been uncertain about their future since a larger round of closures in the 1980s and 1990s, and mainstream schools, as a consequence, have catered for many children who would have formerly attended special schools. There is uncertainty whether this trend will continue. It is also the case that whereas the earlier rounds of inclusion focused on children with moderate learning difficulties and sensory and physical impairments, mainstream schools are now being asked to include more children with severe or complex learning difficulties such as autistic spectrum disorders. Many of these children, although not all, will be working below Level 1 of the National Curriculum and will therefore be assessed on the P scales. The government suggested (DCSF 2007) that most mainstream schools will only have a few children working below Level 1 and in need of assessment on the P scales. Although this may be the case at a national level it overlooks considerable regional, local authority and school based variations in the number of children with more severe SENs included in mainstream schools. It also fails to comment on whether more children with severe and profound learning difficulties are likely to attend mainstream school in the future and therefore add to the number of children mainstream schools will be required to assess using the P scales.

As described elsewhere in this book, P scales have been in use in special schools since the late 1990s and were initiated by a group of special schools who wished to develop meaningful performance criteria for their children. Some schools have queried the relationship between P scales and Individual Education Plans (IEPs). Despite the emphasis on IEPs in the Code of Practice (DfES 2001) more recent DfES directives appear to signal a change in policy. 'It is now government policy that IEPs are only one method by which schools can plan for pupils with SEN' (Leading On Inclusion, DFES 2005). This document goes on to say that, where schools have coherent plans for individually recording the progress of all pupils through personalised learning, IEPs may no longer be necessary.

Rouse and McLaughlin (2007) pointed out that assessment for children with SENs can be debated at both a conceptual and a technical level. At the conceptual level there are concerns about the influence of high stakes assessment on school policy and practice. At a technical level there is concern about the validity of assessment even at National Curriculum levels once individual accommodations or modifications are introduced for children with SENs. Sireci, Li and Scarpatti (2003) found that the impact of a specific accommodation interacted in a unique manner with an individual child's score so that it was not possible to generalise about validity in relation to a particular accommodation. Most of the specific issues relating to P scales, especially in terms of validity and reliability and their application in school are dealt with in Chapter 4 but some aspects of their wider relationship to SEN and overall education policy will be considered here.

SEN Policy and P scales

A fundamental concern is that the government is pursuing both a standards and an inclusion agenda and these are not always compatible. Evidence on this point is mixed, with some arguing that inclusion and high academic standards can go hand in hand (Ainscow 2007), whereas others argue that this is not necessarily the case. Norwich, for example, found that academically successful schools were less likely to include children with Special Educational Needs than less academically successful schools (2002). P scales could be seen as part of an attempt to reconcile these two agendas by enabling schools to record academic progress below Level 1 of the National Curriculum. Ofsted, in their overall judgement of school quality have also increased their emphasis on how effectively mainstream schools meet the needs of SEN children.

Another concern is that, ultimately, P scales may be used to compare performance across schools and contribute to league tables on schools' performance. At present the government says it does not intend to use P scale data as part of any performance tables or to publish data in a form that identifies individual schools. Despite these re-assurances inevitable parallels are drawn to the publishing of National Curriculum test results. Martin (2006) pointed to the following DfES (2005) statement about P scale data to underline his concern on this point.

'The department and OFSTED hope to make use of this national information in future so that schools which use the scales can make meaningful comparisons about the progress made by pupils working below the National Curriculum' (DfES 2005).

In response to this, QCA (2005) stated that P scales were not designed to be used 'as a crude performance indicator for making staff or schools accountable for effectiveness' (p6).

Byers (2003) in his consultative review of P scales noted that 'Respondents are aware of a "fine line" between the uses of data for school self-review and the culture of competition and comparison between schools, based on national data, which they see as wholly inappropriate for special schools and in relation to pupils with SEN in the mainstream' (p17).

Schools seem divided on this issue with some seeing comparability across schools as an asset of P scales and others seeing this as highly undesirable. Much depends on the spirit in which comparability is conducted and the degree of formality involved. It can be argued that, as with their statements on inclusion, government policy in relation to P scales contains some ambiguities and a clearer indication of their role within SEN education is desirable.

Martin (2006) argued that the best fit judgements required when assigning P scale levels are too unreliable and inconsistent to be used for comparing the performance of teachers or schools. Martin is Headteacher of a special school and has carefully researched the use of P scales in his school. In special school settings teachers gain considerable experience of using P scales with a number of children. If, even in these settings, there are difficulties in making best fit judgements, it raises concerns for teachers in mainstream schools who may only use P scales with the occasional child. There is also the investment in time required and the need for adequate resources in terms of training, recording and moderation. It was stressed by the QCA (2007) that teachers need to take context into account when using P scales but questions have to be raised in mainstream schools as to who will be making these P scale observations. In reality much of the one-to-one or small group support for children with more severe Special Educational Needs is delivered by learning support assistants or teaching assistants.

Some of the government documentation does mention classroom support workers in passing but there is little explicit discussion of what their role will be in the use of P scales. This is linked to the more general issue that, often, support workers get to know and work with children with SENs in more depth than classroom teachers. Pscalesmatters (2007) advise that 'for some learners, it may be appropriate to ignore elements of a descriptor to acknowledge the impact of particular impairments'. It is surprising that relatively little has been published on how P scales should be adapted for children with sensory or physical impairments. At present this appears to be left to individual judgements, which means that careful moderation would be needed if these scores are to be made public.

P scales and the Curriculum

A final concern is the relationship between the P scales and curriculum planning and implementation. QCA (2005) stated that P scales should not be used 'to define curriculum content or as a detailed step by step curriculum' (p6). But, as P scales break down overall targets into small steps, there is the possibility that, as these need to be achieved for the child to reach the next level, they will, in effect, shape that part of the curriculum. QCA (2005) acknowledged that P scales only covered National Curriculum areas and that there are other important curriculum areas to be covered for many children with SENs. Despite this acknowledgement, it is easy to envisage that more attention may be given to areas of the curriculum where there is a statutory requirement to record children's progress, even if, for some children, other areas of the curriculum may be far more crucial to their learning. A number of commentators have questioned the appropriateness of the National Curriculum for children with a range of SENs, for example, Lewis and Norwich (2005). Jordan (2005), for example, argued that for many children with Autistic Spectrum Disorders (ASDs) relevance is a more critical aspect of curriculum design than balance. Ware (2005) considered that for children with Profound and Multiple Learning Difficulties (PMLDs) the focus should be on communication and interaction rather than breadth of curriculum, and questioned the relevance of the National Curriculum. Miller and Hodges (2005) criticised the lack of specialised sensory education for deaf blind children. Requiring all children to participate in a National Curriculum or work towards it can be seen as positive as it includes all children in the same learning enterprise. But the problem is that, for some children with SENs, it may not deliver the best and most appropriate education. P scales at their best can be seen as a positive and enabling tool for promoting the learning of children with SENs in an inclusive environment. At their worst they can be seen as a bureaucratic tool that has a negative impact on the curriculum balance required by some children to meet their particular needs.

P scales and the Quality of SEN Education

A concern within SEN education is that since the end of 1980s the focus has been largely on inclusion and that this has dominated the agenda in terms of research, discussion and development. Although much has been written about inclusion, it can be argued that this has inadvertently taken the focus away from the quality of the education that children with SENs receive wherever their school placement. The P scales, despite some drawbacks, can be seen as an opportunity to focus clearly on the quality of their education. It provides a common language and starting point across the whole range of school-age education provision. It should enhance work between special and mainstream schools and allow special schools to share their expertise with mainstream schools. In the future there may need to be more debate about the nature of the curriculum that some children with SENs are required to follow, with attendant adaptation and development of appropriate P scales. In a sense, implementing P scales brings the same advantages and disadvantages that National Curriculum assessment holds for all children. The hallmark of full inclusion may be that the same agenda of target setting, standards and assessment will apply to all children.

References

Ainscow M (2007) From special education to effective schools for all: a review of progress so far. In L Florian (Ed.) *The Sage Handbook of Special Education*. London: Sage.

Byers R (2003) *Developing the P scales: Report and Recommendations to the DfES in Association with QCA*. London: DfES.

DCSF (2007) Explanatory memorandum to the Education National Curriculum Attainment Targets and Programme of Study (England) Amendment Order 2007 No. 2265.

DfE (1994) *Code of Practice on the Identification and Assessment of Special Educational Needs*. Nottingham: DfE. www.dcsf.gov.uk/publications

DfES (1997) *Excellence for all Children*. London: The Stationery Office.

DfES (2001) *Special Educational Needs Code of Practice (Revised)*. London: DfES.

DfES (2004) *Removing Barriers to Achievement – The Government's Strategy for SEN*. Nottingham: DfES publications.

DfES (2005) *Guidance on P scales*. www.qca.org.uk

DfES (2007) *Statistical First Release on Special Educational Needs in England*, London, Department for Education and Skills.

DES (1970) *Education (Handicapped Children) Act*. London: HMSO.

DES (Warnock M) (1978) *Special Educational Needs: Report of the Committee of Enquiry into the education of handicapped young children and people. (The Warnock Report.)* London: HMSO.

DES (1981) *Education Act 1981*. London: HMSO.

Dockrell J and McShane J (1993) *Children's Learning Difficulties: A Cognitive Approach*. Oxford: Blackwell.

Education and Skills Committee (2006) *Special Educational Needs. Third Report of Session 2005–2006, Vol 1*. London: House of Commons.

Frederickson N and Cline T (2002) *Special Educational Needs, Inclusion and Diversity*. Buckingham: Open University Press.

Gutierrez KD and Stone LD (1997) A cultural–historical view of learning and learning disabilities participating in a community of learners. *Learning Disabilities Research and Practice* 12(2), 123–131.

Jordan R (2005) Autistic spectrum disorders. In A Lewis and B Norwich (Eds) *Special Teaching for Special Children?* Maidenhead: Open University Press.

Kiernan C and Riddick B (1973) *A Draft Programme in Operant Techniques, Vol 2*. London: Institute of Education.

Lewis A and Norwich B (2005) (Eds) *Special Teaching for Special Children?* Maidenhead: Open University Press.

Martin A (2006) Assessment using the P scales: best fit-fit for purpose. *British Journal of Special Education* 33(2), 68–75.

Meijer C, Soriano V and Watkins A (2003) *Special Needs Education in Europe.* Brussels: European Agency for Development in Special Needs Education.

Miller O and Hodges L (2005) Deafblindness. In A Lewis and B Norwich (Eds) *Special Teaching for Special Children?* Maidenhead: Open University Press.

Norwich B (2002) Individual differences – Recognising and resolving dilemmas. *British Journal of Educational Studies* 50(4), 482–502.

Norwich B (2007) Categories of special educational needs. In L Florian (Ed.) *The Sage Handbook of Special Education.* London: Sage.

Pscalesmatters (2007) Making best fit judgements by pscalesmatters. http://pscalesmatters.wordpress.com. Accessed 2007/05/09.

QCA (2007) *Using the P scales.* London: Qualifications and Curriculum Authority.

QCA (2005) *Using the P scales.* London: Qualifications and Curriculum Authority.

Riddick B and Kiernan C (1972) *A Draft Programme in Operant Techniques,* Vol 1. London, Institute of Education.

Rouse M and McLaughlin M (2007) Changing perspectives on special education in the evolving context of educational reform. In L Florian (Ed.) *The Sage Handbook of Special Education,* pp 85–106. London: Sage.

Rutter M, Maughan N, Mortimore P and Ouston J (1979) *Fifteen Thousand Hours. Secondary Schools and their Effects on Children.* London: Open Books.

Sireci SG, Li S and Scarpatti S (2003) *The Effect of Test Performance: A Review of the Literature.* (Research Report No. 45) Washington, DC: Board on Testing and Assessment, National Academy of Sciences.

Solity J (1996) Discrepancy definitions of dyslexia – An assessment through teaching approach. *Educational Psychology in Practice* 12(3), 141–151.

Tomlinson S (1982) *A Sociology of Special Education.* London: Routledge & Kegan Paul.

Ware J (2005) Profound and multiple learning difficulties. In A Lewis and B Norwich (Eds) *Special Teaching for Special Children?* Maidenhead: Open University Press.

Wearmouth J (2000) *Special Educational Provision:Meeting the challenge in schools.* Milton Keynes: The Open University.

CHAPTER 3

A Description of the P scales and Their Use in Assessments

Francis Ndaji and Peter Tymms

Since 1998 there has been a statutory requirement of schools to set performance targets as part of the drive to raise educational standards. It was very difficult or almost impossible for special schools to meet this requirement. The attainment levels of their pupils with Special Educational Needs fell well below those measured by the National Curriculum. Teachers in special schools often set zero targets for pupils, knowing that the majority of them could never achieve the levels expected at the end of each Key Stage. However, the publication of the P scales in 1998 and the issuance to schools in 2001 by the DfES/QCA of the booklet *Supporting the Target Setting Process – Guidance for effective target setting for pupils with special educational need* provided a means by which the attainment levels of pupils with Special Educational Needs could be assessed, enabling all schools to set realistic improvement targets.

The P scales were published for use in the assessment of performance and setting of improvement targets for pupils who have Special Educational Needs whether such pupils are found in special or mainstream schools. Although the scales have been in use for some time, they are still unfamiliar to many teachers. Most teachers in special schools use the P scales, but, understandably, many teachers in mainstream schools do not have experience of them. An Ofsted report in 2004 found that almost all special schools used the P scales to assess individual pupils and to set their targets, although difficulties were encountered by some schools whilst trying to set realistic targets for attainment five terms ahead to meet statutory requirements. However, at that time there were no statutory requirements of maintained mainstream schools to set improvement targets for their pupils with Special Educational Needs, even though some of these pupils worked below Level 1 of the National Curriculum and were unlikely to achieve national expectations.

Many mainstream schools did not have pupils with SEN and therefore were unfamiliar with the P scales, but the growing movement towards inclusion, whereby children with Special Educational Needs are educated alongside other children from their community rather than in special schools, has extended the use of the P scales in mainstream schools.

This chapter seeks to introduce the P scales to teachers and teaching assistants and attempts to demonstrate how best to apply the P scales level descriptors in the assessment of pupils. In the following examples we have applied the methods to selected subjects and P levels. The method can then be extended to P levels in other subject areas.

Structure of the P scales by Subject

Essentially the P scales consist of level descriptions for the core subject areas of English, Mathematics, Science and PSHE, although there are P scales for every subject of the National Curriculum such as IT, Geography, Art, History, Music, Design Technology, Religious Education and Modern Foreign languages. However, at the time of writing, the most important scales to schools are those of the core subject areas, and they are the subjects of this book.

In the current version of the P scales, English is divided into five strands, namely, 'Speaking', 'Listening', 'Speaking and listening', 'Reading' and 'Writing'. Mathematics is divided into 'Using and applying', 'Number' and 'Shapes, space and measures'; and Science is divided into 'Scientific enquiry', 'Life processes and living things', 'Materials and their properties' and 'Physical processes'. PSHE has only one strand.

The lowest level of the P scales in all subjects is P1(i). All strands of English, Mathematics and Science with the exception of 'Speaking and listening' have Level 2 of the National Curriculum as their maximum level, 'Speaking' and 'Listening' and PSHE have a maximum level of P8.

Levels P1(i) to P3(ii) of the P scales are generic for all subjects because the descriptions at this level relate to general skills at very early stages of development. They are not subject specific. Levels P4 to P8 and National Curriculum Levels 1 and 2, 1c, 1b, 1a, 2c, 2b and 2a are all subject-specific level descriptors.

The 'Reading' and 'Writing' strands in English, 'Number' and 'Shape, space and measures' strands in Mathematics all have their National Curriculum Levels 1 and 2 divided into 1c, 1b and 1a, and 2c, 2b and 2a in ascending order. On the other hand, the 'Using and applying' in Mathematics, and the Science strands of 'Scientific enquiry', 'Life processes and living things', 'Materials and their properties' and 'Physical processes' all have National Curriculum Levels 1 and 2 that are not subdivided.

Table 3.1: P levels and National Curriculum levels for each subject (current version)

Subjects	Subject strands	P levels and NC levels for each subject
English	Speaking	P1(i) to P8
	Listening	P1(i) to P8
	Speaking and listening	L1c to L2a
	Reading	P1(i) to P8, L1c to L2a
	Writing	P1(i) to P8, L1c to L2a
Mathematics	Using and applying	P1(i) to P8, L1 to L2
	Number	P1(i) to P8, L1c to L2a
	Shape, space and measures	P1(i) to P8, L1c to L2a
Science	Scientific enquiry	P1(i) to P8, L1 to L2
	Life processes and living things	P1(i) to P8, L1 to L2
	Materials and their properties	P1(i) to P8, L1 to L2
	Physical processes	P1(i) to P8, L1 to L2
PSHE and Citizenship	PSHE	P1(i) to P8

Using the P scales for Assessment

What is assessment?

Assessment in the context of the National Curriculum is the process of evaluating a student's achievement on a course of study. Assessment involves the gathering of information on the work a student has done and using the information to determine their achievement on a course. There are several methods through which that information can be obtained. These include tests, examinations, homework, assignments, course work and observation as in the P scales. It is a very important exercise because the results of assessments enable teachers to plan their student's course of learning. The ultimate purpose is to help promote learning.

An assessment can be used for formative or summative purposes. It is formative if it is to be used in the planning of students' future learning steps. A formative assessment is an on-going process in the classroom involving teachers as well as students. A summative assessment is carried out at the end of a course of study or even at the end of a unit of work, to determine the final grades students have achieved.

Identifying the Baseline

The first and probably the most important factor in monitoring the progress of a student is to identify a starting point for learning at the time they enter school. A starting point ensures that there is a baseline against which any progress can be measured and targets for improvement set. A baseline helps teachers to identify their pupils' rate of development, the skills they have acquired, and their level of understanding and knowledge. Setting attainment targets should take all these factors into consideration. Identifying a starting point often involves several professionals including teachers and carers, but there are baseline assessments such as the PIPS On-entry Baseline Assessment (Tymms 1999) that are carried out by the teacher in a relatively short time, usually about 20 minutes, at the start of schooling in mainstream education.

The rate of progress can be very slow for pupils with Special Educational Needs. In many cases, that progress may be signalled by a subtle change in the performance of certain tasks or the response to certain circumstances.

Initial or baseline assessment would ideally include:

- response to certain methods of teaching
- personal interests
- support needs
- strengths and weaknesses
- preferred ways of communicating approval and disapproval
- preferred social interaction.

Assigning P Levels

As they are attainment descriptors, each P level for each subject has several indicators of attainment. Because of the nature of the level descriptors, teachers sometimes find the assigning of attainment levels difficult, and they have not always applied the P scales as they were intended, leading to the award of incorrect P levels to pupils.

This chapter addresses the issues involved in using the P scales for assessment so that schools can use them to:

- provide accurate and consistent assessments of their pupils
- set improvement targets for their pupils

- monitor pupil and whole school performance and progress
- inform parents and carers about the progress of their pupils.

Assessment using the P scales criteria is essentially of the best-fit type. It has to be best-fit because there are several elements in the description of every level of attainment in each subject strand and a pupil may not demonstrate all the elements of any given level. A pupil's work may show evidence of achievement in some of the elements of several different levels in one strand or, in some cases, elements of the same level in more than one strand. A teacher applies best-fit by firstly considering the descriptions in the criteria for all the levels of the subject strand and then assigning to the pupil the level that best describes their work. Essentially, the P level awarded to a pupil's work depends on the teacher's judgement.

Several schools have had problems awarding P levels to pupils if the pupil can perform only some of the tasks prescribed for the level. Hence, teachers have asked questions such as, 'One of my pupils can perform three of the five tasks described for the attainment of P4 in Reading, and one of the tasks described for P5. What P level should I award them in Reading?' This and similar issues need to be addressed.

Teachers have assigned P levels in different ways. Some teachers have assigned levels to pupils' work only when those pupils demonstrated they can do all the tasks in the description of the levels. Other teachers have awarded levels to pupils when they demonstrated they could only carry out some of the tasks of the levels.

There are no standard methods of assessment using the P scales. Teachers apply the descriptors according to their understanding of them. However, they are expected to use their professional judgement during the assessment of their pupils' attainment and progress.

Many pupils achieve several tasks of a P level whilst they still have one or two tasks to complete for the level below. If we were to insist on awarding a P level only when a pupil has completed all the tasks in a level descriptor, the pupil would not be awarded either of the two levels at which they have achieved tasks. On the other hand, we would not indicate their true attainment level if we were to award them a level below these two levels. Therefore, a pupil may not have to demonstrate that they can achieve all the tasks of a P scales level before they can be awarded that level. This raises the question as to how many of the tasks in a level descriptor must a pupil achieve before they can be awarded that level. Our advice is to apply a rule of thumb: *award a level if more than half of the descriptors of that level apply to the pupil's work.*

Judgements of any kind are based on evidence. On what evidence should teachers base their judgement of what level description best fits their pupils' work?

Collecting Evidence to Support Judgement

Adequate supporting evidence is necessary in making a correct decision about the P level that best fits a pupil's work. Evidence on pupils' performance can be collected using various methods and tools. With regard to pupils with Special Educational Needs, their attainment level or progress will be affected by, among other factors, the nature and severity of their Special Educational Needs. Some pupils show little evidence of achievement or progress over a long period of time. They may have to be prompted during the assessment before any meaningful response can be obtained from them. In many cases, the teacher may have to pay great attention in order to be able to detect any response to these promptings. However, adopting a standard method of collecting evidence is key to consistency in assessment. If a standard assessment procedure is adopted by all teachers in a school then a reliable and consistent result becomes possible.

Records are of great importance in the collection of evidence. Teachers are required to keep records of:

- pupils' written or art work
- any comments made by pupils on any issues of interest to them
- any statements from other professionals or parents
- observations made by teachers during class activities
- photographic and video evidence.

Evidence can be built on the strength of the information from these sources. However, it would be very cumbersome and superfluous to consider information from all these sources before making a judgement. Clear evidence from any two of these would be enough to assign a best-fit level to a pupil's work. It is important that staff discuss their observations about pupils' everyday work with their colleagues as such discussions offer further evidence and help in moderating assessments. Any piece of evidence should be dated because a trend may be present and rates of progress could be deduced.

Because the P scales are to be used for summative assessment, evidence should be collected over a period of time and reviewed by teachers together in order to establish whether a pupil's performance over the period under review is enough to award a particular P level. Best-fit judgements can then be arrived at by comparing a pupil's work against items or elements of a level descriptor.

Examples of Evidence Collection

The collation of attainment evidence for pupils with learning difficulty can be achieved in various ways, but often it is in a review setting with the active involvement of the pupil concerned. It is advisable for teachers to organise a session at the end of every week to review a pupil's activities for the week and to verify how much they achieved towards meeting their learning target for the week. It is also important to conduct this review having in mind the context of the targets described in the pupil's annual review planner. Discussions and any amendments to targets must be entered in the appropriate section of the week's record sheet. Since it is, essentially, a review of the passing week, each pupil should be encouraged to discuss their activities over the past week including their likes and dislikes. This weekly review provides a wealth of information and, with the passing of time, yields an extensive profile of the pupil. The profile will, among other things, show the subject areas where the pupil is making more progress and other areas where their progress is not as great and needs more attention from their teachers.

Issues to Consider when Collecting Evidence

When collecting evidence of attainment it is important to bear in mind that because of the circumstances peculiar to each pupil, their performance or response at any one time may be influenced by a variety of factors:

- *Time of day:* Some pupils may prefer morning to afternoon activities. Others may prefer the opposite. However, teachers will identify each pupil's time preference as their profiles continue to be built up.
- *Environment:* Environmental factors such as room setting – the brightness or darkness of the room, the number of people in the room, the level of noise, etc. The teacher will at some point identify a pupil's environmental preferences.
- *Member of staff:* Pupils interact differently with different people and some teachers bring out the best in particular pupils. As professionals, teachers must deal with this issue and make assessments that take this into account.
- *Presence of other pupils:* This may cause discomfort to some pupils, especially if the pupil being assessed has been subjected to any kind of bullying in the school.
- *Particular sensory experience:* This may affect a pupil's response or performance during assessment, especially if they have sensory impairments.
- *Emerging talents in particular subject areas:* These may have a positive or negative impact on a pupil's response or assessment. It will obviously impact positively on a pupil's response if the topic under discussion or review is within the area of the pupil's interest. However, it could have a negative effect because at this level of education there is a danger that a pupil may favour one area and neglect others.
- *Access to favourite items of equipment:* If a pupil fails to obtain their preferred equipment they could become distracted.

It is vital that teachers stay alert to the effect that these factors may have when assessing their pupils. It may be that adjustments are needed so that pupils can be provided with the most convenient setting for their assessments and review sessions.

Attainment below Level 1 of the National Curriculum is difficult to measure. However, it can be measured if there is recognition that the development of internal learning processes is accompanied by increasing attentiveness, discrimination and participation in experiences and activities to which the pupils are exposed. These increases in attention, discrimination and participation give rise to changes in each pupil's responses to events and behaviours as their perceptions and experiences during the learning process develop into specific areas of skills, knowledge and understanding. As they manifest themselves, so the teacher collects evidence. These changes constitute the framework on which the recognition and measurement of attainment can be drawn and it is based on these that the performance descriptions of the P scales have been written.

As noted earlier, the performance descriptors for P1(i) to P3(ii) apply to all subjects as at those levels pupils show general attainment with no subject-specific input.

Levels P1(i) to P3(ii) are the most difficult to measure because at the lowest levels pupil responses can be very subtle. Levels P4 to P8 are subject-specific because at these levels pupils begin to show the acquisition of subject-focused skills and understanding.

Table 3.2 shows the level descriptions for attainment levels from P1(i) to P3(ii).

The descriptions of attainment levels are rather verbose and it can be difficult to identify the key items during the assessment process. In order to conduct a best-fit analysis to ascertain which

Table 3.2: Performance descriptors for P1(i) to P3(ii)

P1(i)

Pupils encounter activities and experiences. They may be passive or resistant. They may show simple reflex responses, for example, startling at sudden noises or movements. Any participation is fully prompted.

P1(ii)

Pupils show emerging awareness of activities and experiences. They may have periods when they appear alert and ready to focus their attention on certain people, events, objects or parts of objects, *for example, attending briefly to interactions with a familiar person.* They may give intermittent reactions, *for example, sometimes becoming excited in the midst of social activity.*

P2(i)

Pupils begin to respond consistently to familiar people, events and objects. They react to new activities and experiences, for example, withholding their attention. They begin to show interest in people, events and objects, for example, smiling at familiar people. They accept and engage in coactive exploration, for example, focusing their attention on sensory aspects of stories or rhymes when prompted.

Table 3.2: *Continued*

P2(ii)

Pupils begin to be proactive in their interactions. They communicate consistent preferences and affective responses, *for example, reaching out to a favourite person.* They recognise familiar people, events and objects, *for example, vocalising or gesturing in a particular way in response to a favourite visitor.* They perform actions, often by trial and improvement, and they remember learned responses over short periods of time, *for example, showing pleasure each time a particular puppet character appears in a poem dramatised with sensory cues.* They co-operate with shared exploration and supported participation, *for example, taking turns in interactions with a familiar person, imitating actions and facial expressions.*

P3(i)

Pupils begin to communicate intentionally. They seek attention through eye contact, gesture or action. They request events or activities, *for example, pointing to key objects or people.* They participate in shared activities with less support. They sustain concentration for short periods. They explore materials in increasingly complex ways, *for example, reaching out and feeling for objects as tactile cues to events.* They observe the results of their own actions with interest, *for example, listening to their own vocalisations.* They remember learned responses over more extended periods, *for example, following the sequence of a familiar daily routine and responding appropriately.*

P3(ii)

Pupils use emerging conventional communication. They greet known people and may initiate interactions and activities, *for example, prompting another person to join in with an interactive sequence.* They can remember learned responses over increasing periods of time and may anticipate known events, *for example, pre-empting sounds or actions in familiar poems.* They may respond to options and choices with actions or gestures, *for example, by nodding or shaking their heads.* They actively explore objects and events for more extended periods, *for example, turning the pages in a book shared with another person.* They apply potential solutions systematically to problems, for example, *bringing an object to an adult in order to request a new activity.*

Source: QCA website at http://www.qca.org.uk/qca_11981.aspx

P level best describes the work of a pupil, it is useful to have a list of the key items/tasks in the description of each level. This makes it easier to identify the tasks pupils have performed and the level they have achieved. An example is given below.

The key items in the P level descriptors for P1(i) to P3(ii) are shown in Table 3.3.

After listing the key elements of the level descriptors, evidence collected from the pupils' work can then be inspected alongside the

Table 3.3: Key items in the descriptors for P1(i) to P3(ii)

P level	Key items of the descriptors
P1(i)	• Shows simple reflexes
	• Participates in activities only when prompted
P1(ii)	• Shows emerging awareness of activities and experiences
	• Shows periodic alertness and readiness to focus on people, events or objects
	• Reacts intermittently, e.g. showing surprise at the sudden presence or absence of a person, an object or event
P2(i)	• Responds consistently to familiar people, events and objects
	• Reacts to new activities
	• Shows interest in people, events and objects
	• Takes part in activities with other pupils
P2(ii)	• Proactive
	• Communicates consistent preferences
	• Recognises familiar people, events, objects
	• Remembers learned responses
	• Co-operates with shared exploration and supported participation
P3(i)	• Communicates intentionally
	• Seeks attention by eye contact, gesture or action
	• Requests events or activities
	• Participates in shared activities without support
	• Sustains concentration for short periods
	• Explores materials and observes the results of their actions
	• Remembers learned responses over more extended periods
P3(ii)	• Communicates conventionally
	• Greets known people and initiates interactions
	• Remembers learned responses over increasing period of time
	• Responds to options and choices
	• Applies potential solutions systematically to problems

list of key elements to identify the P level that has key items that best fit the evidence collected.

A Year 3 Class Scenario

Claire and her friends were seated in their classroom for a Numeracy class. The teacher opened the door and walked in with some pencils, erasers, sheets of paper and plastic cubes. As soon as Ken saw the teacher he started humming a song, though his voice was barely audible. This happened to be a song about numbers that the teacher had sung to draw their attention in the previous lesson. Claire did not seem to have seen the teacher because her attention was focused on a bright red car that was being parked in the car park a few yards from the classroom window. Probably she thought that it was her father's car coming to pick her up from school because her father had a red car. However, Claire turned her attention to the teacher when the teacher banged her hand on the desk to distract her attention from the car. Jimmy reached out for the pencils the teacher had in her hand and some of them dropped on the floor. He was surprised and embarrassed but he picked up these pencils one at a time and placed each of them on the teacher's desk. As soon as a teaching assistant walked into the class, Jimmy beckoned to her by raising his forefinger. The teaching assistant offered him a blue and a yellow pen and Jimmy accepted the yellow one. Kim smiled at the teacher and started playing with the plastic cubes the teacher had brought, creating three columns from the cubes by placing the rest on the three cubes she had used as the bases for the columns, interchanging the colours from time to time to create colour effect. Ken joined Kim to arrange and rearrange the plastic cubes on the floor. He played with only the red cubes though other colours were available to him. Sonia was silent throughout the lesson except when she cried when she was moved to another position to create space at the centre of the room.

In order to award P levels to the pupils involved in the scenario an exercise is conducted to obtain evidence that will adequately describe each pupil's work.

The achievements and targets of the group can be seen in Table 3.4.

Table 3.4: Items achieved by each pupil, levels awarded and targets set for them

Pupil name	Evidence gathered (The level attached to each item is the level at which it is a key item.)	P level awarded	Target
Claire	• Focused on the car – P1(ii) • Passive to teacher's entry – P1(i) • Participated when prompted – P1(i) • Showed simple reflexes – P1(i)	P1(i)	(1) Encounter activities and experiences – P1(i) (2) Intermittent reactions – P1(ii)
Ken	• Responded to familiar people – P2(i) • Reacted to new activities – P2(i) • Took part in activities with others – P2(i) • Showed interest in objects – P2(i)	P2(i)	Ken's targets would be the descriptors in level P2(ii)
Jimmy	• Recognised teacher and teaching assistant – P2(ii) • Communicated intentionally – P3(i) • Acted proactively in replacing the pencils – P2(ii) • Communicated preferred choice – P2(ii)	P2(ii)	(1) Co-operate with shared exploration – P2(ii) (2) All items in P3(i) apart from 'Communicates intentionally', which Jimmy already does
Kim	• Communicated intentionally (by smiling) – P3(i) • Sustained concentration – P3(i) • Participated in shared activities – P3(i) • Explored materials (colours) – P3(i) • Sought attention – P3(i)	P3(i)	(1) Request events – P3(i) (2) Remember learned responses – P3(i) (3) All items in P3(ii)
Sonia	• Passive – P1(i) • Showed reflexes – P1(i)	P1(i)	(1) Encounter activities and experiences – P1(i) (2) All items in P1(ii)

Reasons for awarding the P levels

Claire: Claire was awarded P1(i) because she performed the primary element in the level description for P1(i). She already demonstrated one of the elements in P1(ii) but there are two remaining. Therefore her targets are the remaining two items on P1(ii).

Ken: Ken was awarded P2(i) because he demonstrated the ability to perform all the items in the P2(i) level description. The target set for Ken are the items in the level description for the next level, P2(ii).

Jimmy: Jimmy demonstrated the ability to perform all but one of the four items for P level P2(ii) level descriptors. He also demonstrates the ability to perform one of the P3(i) items. Therefore he has been awarded P2(ii). His targets are to perform the remaining P2(ii) item and all but one of the items in the descriptors for P3(i).

Kim: Kim demonstrated the ability to perform five of the seven items on the P level descriptors for P3(i). She has therefore been awarded P3(i). Targets set for her include the acquisition of the ability to perform the remaining items of P3(i).

Sonia: Sonia has been awarded P1(i) because she was passive. She had to be awarded this level because there is no lower P level. Targets have been set for her to demonstrate the items of P1(i) and P1(ii).

Our approach to the best-fit exercise does not require a pupil to demonstrate the ability to perform all the tasks on a level before they are awarded that level. Some of the pupils have been awarded a P level despite the fact that they have done only some of the tasks in the level descriptors for those P levels. For example, Kim did only five of the seven items in P3(i) and was awarded P3(i). Although no rule stipulates that a pupil must demonstrate ability for all items of a level in order to be deemed to have attained the level, it is important that the pupil demonstrates the ability to perform more than half of the items that describe a level awarded to them, otherwise they must be awarded the next lower level if they demonstrate ability for that lower level. It must be borne in mind that we are registering the level the pupils have attained or are working on. It is important to note that the scenario described above has only been used to demonstrate how P levels should be awarded. There is no guarantee that any of those pupils will display the same abilities on every occasion. However, the teacher knows each pupil personally and is in a good position to say what abilities each child has demonstrated during the period under review.

Best-Fit for Levels P4 to P8 in Number

The performance descriptors for levels P4 to P8 in Number in the P scales are as shown in Table 3.5.

The key items in the level descriptors for P4 to P8 in Number are shown in Table 3.6.

Table 3.5: Performance descriptors for P4 to P8 in Number

P4

Pupils show an awareness of number activities and counting, *for example, copying some actions during number rhymes, songs and number games; following a sequence of pictures or numbers as indicated by a known person during number rhymes and songs.*

P5

Pupils respond to, and join in with, familiar number rhymes, stories, songs and games, *for example, using a series of actions during the singing of a familiar song; joining in by saying, signing or indicating at least one of the numbers in a familiar number rhyme.* Pupils can indicate one or two, *for example, by using eyepointing, blinks, gestures or any other means to indicate one or two, as required.* They demonstrate that they are aware of contrasting quantities, *for example, 'one' and 'lots' by making groups of one or lots of food items on plates.*

P6

Pupils demonstrate an understanding of one-to-one correspondence in a range of contexts, *for example, matching objects such as cups to saucers, straws to drink cartons.* Pupils join in rote counting up to five, *for example, saying or signing number names to five in counting activities.* They count reliably to three, make sets of up to three objects and use numbers to three in familiar activities and games, *for example, touching one, two, three items as an adult counts, counting toys or pictures, counting out sets of three, e.g. knife, fork and spoon.* They demonstrate an understanding of the concept of more, *for example, indicating that more cups, counters, food items are required.* They join in with new number rhymes, songs, stories and games. Activities should include the use of money as an important context for number development.

Table 3.5: *Continued*

P7

Pupils join in rote counting to 10, *for example, saying or signing number names to 10 in counting activities.* They can count at least five objects reliably, *for example, candles on a cake, bricks in a tower.* They recognise numerals from one to five and understand that each represents a constant number or amount, *for example, putting correct number of objects (1–5) into containers marked with the numeral; collecting the correct number of items up to five.* Pupils demonstrate an understanding of 'less', *for example, indicating which bottle has less water in it.* In practical situations they respond to 'add one' to a number of objects, *for example, responding to requests such as add one pencil to the pencils in the pot, add one sweet to the dish.*

P8

Pupils join in with rote counting to beyond 10, *for example, they say or sign number names in counting activities.* They continue to rote count onwards from a given small number, *for example, continuing the rote count onwards in a game using dice and moving counters up to 10; continuing to say, sign or indicate the count aloud when adult begins counting the first two numbers.* Pupils recognise differences in quantity, *for example, in comparing given sets of objects and saying which has more or less, which is the bigger or smaller group.* They recognise numerals from one to nine and relate them to sets of objects, *for example, labelling sets of objects with correct numerals.* In practical situations they respond to 'add one' to or 'take one away' from a number of objects, *for example, adding one more to three objects in a box, and saying, signing or indicating how many are now in the box; at a cake sale saying, signing or indicating how many cakes are left when one is sold.* They use ordinal numbers (first, second, third) when describing the position of objects, people or events, *for example, indicating who is first in a queue or line; who is first, second and third in a race or competition.* Pupils estimate a small number (up to 10) and check by counting, *for example, suggesting numbers that can be checked by counting, guessing then counting the number of: pupils in a group; adults in the room; cups needed at break time.*

Source: QCA website at http://www.qca.org.uk/qca_11977.aspx

Table 3.6: Key items in the level descriptors for P4 to P8 in Number

P level	Key items of the descriptors
P4	• Copies actions during number rhymes, songs and number games • Follows sequences of pictures or numbers during number rhymes and songs
P5	• Responds to, and joins in, with familiar number rhymes, stories and songs using actions during singing • Joins in by saying, signing or indicating at least one of the numbers in a familiar number rhyme • Indicates one or two by eye-pointing, blinks or gestures • Demonstrates awareness of contrasting quantities, e.g. one and lots
P6	• Demonstrates an understanding of one-to-one correspondence • Rote-counts up to five • Reliably counts up to three, makes sets of up to three objects and uses numbers up to three in activities • Understands the concept of 'more'
P7	• Rote-counts up to 10 • Reliably counts up to five objects • Recognises numerals from one to five • Understands the concept of 'less' • Understands the concept of increment
P8	• Rote-counts beyond 10 • Continues the rote-count onwards when an adult begins the counting • Recognises differences in quantity • Recognises numerals from one to nine and relates them to objects • Responds to 'add one' or 'take one away' • Uses ordinal numbers when describing positions, e.g. first or second in a queue, etc. • Estimates a small number and checks by counting

A Year 5 Class Scenario

In a Year 5 Numeracy class to teach pupils the concept of Numbers, the teacher demonstrated counting up to 10 by singing a popular song that most of the pupils seemed to have enjoyed previously. The song, *Show me your number*, usually stopped each time the teacher called out a number. Before the song started each pupil was given 12 coloured crayons and was required to indicate that they knew the number called out by the teacher by holding up the corresponding number of crayons. The teacher checked the number of crayons each pupil had in their hand. The teacher then asked the pupils to either add or discard one or two crayons and after that asked how many were left in their hand. Before the song was re-started, pupils were asked to keep in a box the crayons they had shown to the teacher. At intervals the teacher went round asking each pupil whether they had more crayons in their box or in their original pool of crayons.

All pupils with the exception of Alice and James joined in the singing. Harry sang but could not show the correct number of crayons when the teacher called out a number higher than one. Mary, Sheila, Andy and Mark each took part in the singing. Mary correctly indicated numbers one and two but could not say whether she had more or less crayons in her hand than in the pool. Mary got it right when the teacher said to her 'Give me one crayon' and 'Give me many crayons'. Sheila correctly indicated up to five during singing, knew, when asked, whether she had more or less numbers of crayons in her hand than in her pool and put three crayons in a box when asked to do so. Andy correctly indicated up to six during the song and, when asked to remove two crayons from the six he had in his hands, did so correctly. He also knew, when asked, whether he had more or less crayons in his left hand than in his right hand and successfully increased the crayons in his left hand by one when asked to do so.

On the next day the class started with a rote-counting exercise to determine to what extent each pupil could rote-count. The teacher conducted the exercise by asking the class to sing number rhymes a few times and observed each pupil. By observing each pupil the teacher found that Harry and Mary could rote-count up to three. Sheila could rote-count up to six while Andy could rote-count up to 12.

After the singing session the teacher wrote numbers from 1 to 10 on the small whiteboard in the classroom and distributed some coloured plastic animal toys to the pupils for them to count with her.

It was Sheila's birthday and her mother brought her birthday cake with candles on it to the class so that her friends could join in her birthday celebration. When asked to count the candles on her birthday cake Sheila counted up to four and stopped, but she recognised from one to six on the small whiteboard. Sheila added one to the four candles when the teacher told her that she wanted more candles.

When asked to count her plastic animals Mary could count only one of 11 and she could not identify any of the numbers on the board when it was brought near to her. Andy counted his toys up to eight and identified one to six out of the numbers on the white board. The teacher was aware that in previous lessons Emma had done all the things Andy was now doing and, in addition, could recognise numbers 1 to 10 on the white board and count beyond 10, but she could not do other tasks required for level P8.

The teacher asked the pupils to queue up in front of the class to hand back their crayons. He then asked each of them, separately, who is first, second and third in the queue. Of all the pupils only Andy could answer correctly.

The achievements and targets of the group can be seen in Table 3.7.

Harry: Harry was awarded P4 because he demonstrated the ability to perform all items of P4 descriptors. His next targets are P5 descriptors.

Mary: Mary demonstrated ability to perform three of the four level descriptors of P5. She has been awarded P5. Her target is to perform the one unaccomplished P5 descriptor and all the items of level P6.

Sheila: Sheila demonstrated ability for three of the four items in the P6 descriptors and has therefore been awarded P6. She also demonstrated ability for one item in level P7. Sheila's targets are the P6 item she has yet to perform and all the items of P7 except the one she has completed.

Table 3.7: Items achieved by each pupil, levels awarded and targets set

Pupil name	*Evidence gathered* *(The levels attached to each item is the level at which it is a key item.)*	*P level awarded*	*Target*
Harry	• Copied actions during number rhymes –P4 • Followed in singing the number rhymes – P4	P4	All items of P5
Mary	• Responded to number rhymes – P5 • Indicated one and two – P5 • Demonstrates awareness of quantities – P5	P5	(1) Indicate one or two by eye pointing, blinking or other gestures – P5 (2) All items of P6 descriptors
Sheila	• Rote-counted up to five – P6 • Understood the concept of 'more'– P6 • Applied numbers up to four in activities – P6 • Recognised numerals from one to six – P7	P6	(1) Understand one to one correspondence – P6 (2) All items of P7 except 'recognises numerals from one to six'
Andy	• Rote-counted up to twelve – P8 • Reliably counted up to eight – P7 • Recognised numerals from one to six – P7 • Understood the concept of less – P7 • Understood the concept of increment – P7 • Used ordinal numbers – P8	P7	All items of P8 except the two in which he has demonstrated ability
Emma	• Could do all the things Andy could do except the P8 items – P7 • Recognised numerals from 1 to 10 – P8 • Counted beyond 10 – P7	P7	All items of P8 except 'Recognise numerals from one to nine' and 'Count beyond 10

Andy: Andy has been awarded P7 because he demonstrated ability for all items of level P7 descriptors. In fact for two of the descriptors he was already working on level P8. He has been set a target of the P8 descriptors except for the two items of P8 for which he has already demonstrated ability.

Emma: In a previous class Emma had done all the P7 items that Andy had done and had also accomplished two items of level P8. Therefore she has been awarded P7. Her target is all the P8 descriptors except those for which she has already demonstrated ability.

Best-fit for Levels P4 to P8 in Reading

The performance descriptors for P4 to P8 in Reading are shown in Table 3.8.

The key items in the P level descriptors for P4 to P8 in Reading are shown in Table 3.9.

Table 3.8: Items achieved by each pupil, levels awarded and targets set

P4

Pupils listen and respond to familiar rhymes and stories. They show some understanding of how books work, *for example, turning pages and holding the book the right way up.*

P5

Pupils select a few words, symbols or pictures with which they are particularly familiar and derive some meaning from text, symbols or pictures presented in a way familiar to them. They match objects to pictures and symbols, *for example choosing between two symbols to select a drink or seeing a photograph of a child and eye-pointing at the child.* They show curiosity about content at a simple level, for example they may answer basic two key-word questions about a story.

P6

Pupils select and recognise or read a small number of words or symbols linked to a familiar vocabulary, *for example, name, people, objects or actions. They match letters and short words.*

Table 3.8: *Continued*

P7

Pupils show an interest in the activity of reading. They predict elements of a narrative, *for example, when the adult stops reading, pupils fill in the missing word.* They distinguish between print or symbols and pictures in texts. They understand the conventions of reading, *for example, following text left to right, top to bottom and page following page.* They know that their name is made up of letters. The prediction can be demonstrated in any mode of communication used by the child.

P8

Pupils understand that words, symbols and pictures convey meaning. They recognise or read a growing repertoire of familiar words or symbols, including their own names. They recognise at least half the letters of the alphabet by shape, name or sound. They associate sounds with patterns in rhymes, with syllables, and with words or symbols. While letter sounds can be taught in all sorts of imaginative ways, their learning should not be emphasised at the expense of developing Speaking and Listening.

Source: QCA website at http://www.qca.org.uk/qca_11981.aspx

Table 3.9: Key items in the level descriptors of P4 to P8 in Reading

P level	Key items of the descriptors
P4	• Listens and responds to familiar rhymes and stories • Understands how books work
P5	• Selects familiar words, symbols or pictures • Derives some meaning from text, symbols and pictures • Matches objects to pictures and symbols • Shows curiosity about content
P6	• Selects and recognises or reads small numbers of words or symbols linked to a familiar vocabulary • Matches letters and short words
P7	• Shows interest in reading • Distinguishes between print or symbols and pictures • Understands reading conventions, e.g. left to right, top to bottom • Knows that names are made of letters
P8	• Understands that words, symbols and pictures convey meaning • Recognises or reads familiar words or symbols including their own names • Recognises at least half the letters of the alphabet by shape, name or sound

A Year 8 Reading Class Scenario

The English language teacher walked into the classroom for a Reading lesson with Year 8 pupils with special educational needs (SEN). He brought with him a few story books and a tape recorder with recorded rhymes. Some of the pupils were excited on seeing the teacher walk into the class. Others showed no interest and seemed not to care whether he was there or not. One of the excited pupils was Ben. He joined in as the tape recorder played his familiar rhymes and beckoned to the teacher to give him one of the story books. The teacher obliged him. Ben held the book in the right way up and opened it, though it was not certain that he could read. When the teacher took Ben's book and intentionally placed it upside down Ben replaced it correctly. He repeated this with a few other books. However, Ben could not identify words. Before the teacher continued the process with Aisha he gave other pupils some toys to play with.

The teacher gave one of the books to Aisha. She held the book the right way up and opened it just as Ben had done. Aisha pointed at words from left to right identifying and pronouncing chair, spoon, cup. Obviously those were familiar words to her. She also pointed at words on the right-hand page. She pointed to her name on a list given to her by the teacher and matched a picture of a bicycle to that of a man riding a bicycle in the book she held.

David did most of the things Ben and Aisha had done when asked by the teacher, but in addition he read selected sentences one of which he read aloud saying 'Give me the cup' and at the same time lifted the plastic cup he had just used to drink water as a demonstration of the meaning of what he read. When the teacher asked him to pick letters from a mixture of words and numbers to form his name, David did so correctly. The teacher asked him to identify the letters of the alphabet as he pointed to them one at a time. David identified most of the letters.

Maria could do almost all of the things Ben, Aisha and David did. Maria was very excited when the teacher gave her a book. She could read from left to right and top to bottom and could also turn from one page to another. When asked to do so she created her name from a collection of letters mixed with numerals.

After reading some pages of one of the story books with Okon, the teacher turned to a page and asked Okon to pronounce some words as he pointed to them. Okon pronounced some of them correctly. The teacher opened another page and called out words one after the other asking Okon to identify each as he called it out. Okon was again successful. The teacher gave Okon pictures of various activities (e.g. pupils playing football, a girl eating, a man running, etc.) and called out the activities one after the other. Okon picked pictures corresponding to each activity. He also identified most of the letters of the alphabet.

When given the book by the teacher Rachel did not show any interest. She had to be persuaded to hold the book and did not show any interest in the instructions the teacher was giving her.

Amina was very enthusiastic as shown in the readiness with which she responded when the teacher asked to read the book with her. After reading a few pages with the teacher she was able to identify some of the words they had read as the teacher called them out. She could also read aloud a number of words on one page.

The achievements and targets of the group can be seen in Table 3.10.

Ben: Ben demonstrated ability for all the items in P4 but could not perform any items of higher levels. He was therefore awarded P4 with the target to work hard to perform the items on level P5.

Aisha: Aisha performed all P4 items and three of the four items of P5. She also demonstrated ability for one of the items in P8. She was awarded P5. Her target is to perform the one item of P5 she is yet to perform and all items of P6.

David: David performed all items in level P6 and one item in P8. He was awarded P6. His target is to perform all items in P7.

Maria: Maria was awarded P7 because she demonstrated ability in three of the four items in level P7. She also demonstrated ability in one item of P8. A target was set for her to perform the one item of level P7 and the items of P8 she has yet to perform.

Okon: Okon demonstrated ability in all the items of level P8 and has therefore been awarded level P8. He was set a target to perform all items of the next higher level which is National Curriculum Level 1c.

Table 3.10: Items achieved by each pupil in Reading, levels awarded and targets set

Pupil Name	Evidence gathered *(The level attached to each item is the level at which it is a key item.)*	P level awarded	Target
Ben	• Responded to familiar rhymes – P4 • Understood how books work – P4	P4	All items of P5
Aisha	• Did all that Ben did (above) – P4 • Selected familiar words – P5 • Matched objects to pictures – P5 • Derived meaning from text – P5 • Pointed at her name in a list – P8	P5	(1) Show curiosity about content – P5 (2) All items of P6
David	• Did all that Ben and Aisha did (above) – P4 and P5 • Recognised and read small sentences – P6 • Matched letters and words – P6 • Identified most letters of the alphabet – P8	P6	All items of P7
Maria	• Did all that Ben, Aisha and David did (above) – P6 • Showed interest in reading – P7 • Understood reading conventions – P7 • Knew that names are made of letters – P7	P7	(1) Distinguish between print and pictures – P7 (2) All items of P8
Okon	• Understood that words and symbols convey meaning – P8 • Recognised and read familiar words – P8 • Recognised most of the alphabet – P8	P8	All items of National Curriculum Level 1c

The best-fit examples described above are demonstrations of how the authors think the exercise should be carried out. A few cases were selected to cover the P levels ranging from P1 to P8 in Reading and Number, but the method can be applied to other subjects. It is clear from the examples, that in order to carry out pupils' assessment in any subject using the P scales, the teacher must first prepare a list of the key items or tasks from the descriptors of each level. A pupil should demonstrate the ability to perform at least half of these tasks in order to be awarded a level in the given subject. The evidence is then matched against the key items to find out which P level the pupil's evidence best describes. It must be emphasised that consistency in the application of any rule or method is the key to the collection of reliable data.

Recognition of Progress

The previous section described the assessment of pupils' work in order to determine their attainment levels in various subjects and to provide information about how well they are performing. Progress information is used in feeding back to parents/guardians, setting pupil improvement targets, setting school targets, etc. The importance of identifying progress cannot be overemphasised.

In general, progress is about change and pupil development and this is the case whether the pupil is in a mainstream or a special school. Most pupils with Special Educational Needs can demonstrate progress through increased knowledge, skills and understanding. Although they follow the same progress pattern as their fellow pupils who do not have a Special Educational Need, their progress may not occur at the same age or rate. In addition, a pupil may progress in certain curriculum areas but not in others. For example, a pupil may show progress in English but not in Mathematics, and vice versa.

Recognition and identification of progress is more difficult in pupils who are working at the very low levels of the P scales; that is, pupils who are working in the range of P1(i) to P3(ii). Indication of progress at such low levels may be very subtle. The following examples may be useful.

- A pupil has made progress if they develop responses to certain actions, events or experiences where previously they made none.
- A pupil has made progress if their dependence on others is reduced.
- A pupil has made progress if the need to have normal school activities made available to them in a personalised way is reduced.
- A pupil has made progress if the frequency of any undesirable behaviour is reduced.

Identification and recognition of progress in pupils working at level P4 of the P scales and above are subject-specific and are usually measured using the increase in the pupils' subject attainment levels.

Areas of Potential Problems When Recording P scales Attainments

The P scales have been revised occasionally but experience has shown that teachers are often unaware of changes, continuing to use the old criteria even after they have been replaced with new versions. For example, in the current version of the P scales, English has the strands 'Speaking', 'Listening', 'Reading' and 'Writing'. In the current version 'Speaking' has P levels from P1(i) to P8, as does 'Listening'. The rule is that a pupil whose attainment level in 'Speaking' or in Listening' is above P8 should have their score recorded in a combined 'Speaking and listening' strand. Therefore, if a pupil's score in 'Speaking' or in 'Listening' is National Curriculum Level 1c or above, they should not be given P level scores in 'Speaking' or in 'Listening'. However, many teachers do not apply this rule; instead they continue to award levels above P8 in 'Speaking' and in 'Listening'. It is also incorrect to award levels P8 or lower to pupils in the combined 'Speaking and listening'.

It is important to note that:

1. in Mathematics, the 'Using and applying' strand has levels P1(i) to L1 of the National Curriculum. L1 is not split into L1c, L1b and L1a as is the case in 'Number' and 'Shape, space and measure' that also have levels P1(i) to L2a.

2. the Science strands all have the maximum level of L2 of the National Curriculum. The levels L1 and L2 here are not split into sub-levels.
3. some teachers still award levels higher than P8 in PSHE. This subject has a maximum score of P8 in the current version of the P scales assessment criteria.

Some teachers when recording P scales data continue to enter W (working towards Level 1) in some subjects for some of their pupils. It must be remembered that the P scales were established in order that W would no longer be used as a performance indicator for pupils working below National Curriculum Level 1.

Of course, further changes are likely to be made to the P scales but it is hoped that future alterations will be small.

Moderation

The need to conduct moderation exercises was identified by the DfES in the early 2000s when it was found that schools were applying the P scales criteria in different ways. In fact, the application of the P scales criteria within some schools varied from one teacher to another. However, it is noteworthy that teachers recognised the need for common standards across schools as indicated in the P scales consultation report of 2007. The Qualifications and Curriculum Authority (QCA) had earlier recognised this need and, in response, held moderation exercises in several cities in England with the intention of unifying the approaches taken by teachers when using the P scales criteria and to set standards for assessment. The overall aim was to ensure that a pupil's work awarded P5 in Reading in School X will also be awarded P5 in School Y. Similar moderation exercises at regional, LA and school levels from time to time are advisable in order to ensure consistency in assessment methods and standards.

Reference

Tymms P (1999) *Baseline Assessment and Monitoring in Primary Schools.* London: David Fulton.

Further Reading

National Curriculum online. Recognising progress and achievement. http://www.nc.uk.net/ld/GG_recog.html.

http://www.qca.org.uk/qca_11981.aspx.

QCA (2007) *P scales consultation report.* March 2007. http://www.qca.org. uk

CHAPTER 4

Reliability and Validity of the P scales Data

Francis Ndaji and Peter Tymms

The two most common questions asked about a measuring instrument or a test system are: (1) Is it reliable? and (2) Is it valid? This chapter considers the quality of the P scales data in relation to their reliability and validity.

Reliability

Reliability, for our purposes, refers to the consistency of a set of data, a measuring instrument or a test system. It addresses the issue of whether the same results would be produced each time a test or measure was administered to the same person under the same conditions. A very reliable measuring instrument would be expected to give the same reading each time it is applied to a measurement. In practice, in educational assessment, we do not expect to get the same results each time, but we do expect some degree of consistency.

A reliable test must prove that if it were taken by similar pupils under similar conditions, similar results would be obtained. It should also demonstrate that if the same pupils were re-tested it would yield similar results provided an appropriate length of time was chosen between test and re-test. For the P scales, retesting by the same person would not make much sense because a teacher could simply be recording their own opinion twice.

The P scales system would be judged to be reliable if, for example, a pupil scored P7 in Speaking no matter which teacher conducted the assessment. It would also be judged to be reliable if similar pupils (i.e. pupils of the same ability, age and Special Educational Need) scored the same P level no matter which teacher conducted the assessment, or, if similar pupils scored the same P level when assessed by the same teacher. However, if using the P scales assessment criteria, different teachers scored different P levels for a pupil under the same conditions, there would be a problem.

How can We Measure Reliability of the P scales Assessment Criteria?

In general it is not possible to measure reliability in absolute terms, but an estimate of reliability can be obtained using any of the methods described below.

Test–retest reliability

Test–retest reliability assumes the consistency of a test over time when there is no change in the quality being measured. A test is administered at two different points in time and the results examined to determine the level of consistency. For example, a set of pupils with learning difficulties can be assessed using an appropriate test by a teacher who knows them well and re-assessed after a few months by a different teacher who, again, knows the pupils well. The ability of the pupils would not have changed drastically within those few months, therefore the extent to which the two sets of results agree could be used to determine the reliability of the assessment criteria over time. Test–retest reliability has been the subject of much criticism by researchers of the opinion that a short period between tests could yield erroneously high estimates of reliability. Other critics maintain that a long interval between tests could produce an erroneous result because of maturation. It is important that an appropriate interval is chosen, one that is neither too long nor too short. Test–retest reliability tests apply to paper-based tests. However, as the P scales are teacher ratings, a teacher reassessing the same pupil may be influenced by earlier performance.

Inter-rater reliability

The inter-rater reliability test is used to assess the consistency of teachers in the application of a test. In other words, it will ascertain that the same methods and standards are being applied in the conduct of the test. For example, we know that the P scales assessment is essentially a best-fit judgement. The inter-rater reliability would determine whether different teachers applying the same methods and standards in the assessment of pupils come to the same conclusion.

Inter-rater reliability could be assessed by comparing the P scales scores given by two or more teachers to determine their consistency. For example, the teachers could be asked to assess pupils' work using the P scales assessment criteria and the correlation between the two ratings used to estimate inter-rater reliability. An alternative method could be to have as many teachers as possible determine the pupils' P level scores. The percentage of agreement on a particular P level would give the inter-rater reliability rate. For example, if the teachers agree in 7 out of 10 cases, then the inter-rater reliability is 70%.

A very practical way to measure teacher reliability is to have a number of teachers (10 or more) assess a number of pupils in various subjects within a reasonable period of time and have the results examined to determine the number of cases in which all the teachers awarded the same P level to all pupils. The percentage of cases where a pupil is awarded the same P level on a subject by all the teachers would give an estimate of teacher reliability on the P scales for that subject.

It would be useful, following this exercise, to discuss the cases where different P levels were awarded, with each teacher giving reasons why they awarded a particular level. In this way assessment standards could be established within the school. This exercise could also be undertaken at Local Authority level.

Internal consistency reliability

Internal consistency reliability measures the consistency across items in the same test. This type of reliability compares test items designed to measure the same area of achievement. The comparison is based on the correlation between the test items. The test is said to have internal consistency if the comparison shows that the items actually measure the same thing.

Causes of Unreliability of Data

In general, any observed score consists of two components, namely, the true score and the error, the error being that component of the score that is attributable to the uncertainty associated with the assessment process. The error is itself made up of two components, the systematic or non-random error and the random error. The systematic or non-random error is related to the method used and is associated with bias. The random error arises from personal or subject mistakes. The greater the error component of the measurement or score the lower its reliability.

In pupil assessment using the P scales, the total error in the score is the sum of the error due to the P scales criteria being unable to measure pupils' scores accurately and the error caused by the teachers applying the criteria incorrectly. Here, the error inherent in the P scales criteria constitutes the systematic or non-random error as does any bias the teacher may have. The error caused by the inaccuracy of judgements constitutes the random error. Much of the systematic error is constant because it is inherent in the system. However, the random error will vary from one teacher to another.

Validity

Validity, for our purposes, is the extent to which a test measures what it was designed to measure. Valid data is data that measures what it was intended to measure. For example, the level descriptions for the subject 'Speaking' in the P scales would be judged valid if they actually measured the speaking ability of pupils. If the level descriptions for 'Speaking' in the P scales did not measure the ability of pupils to speak, then the P scales assessment criteria for 'Speaking' would not be valid.

Several types of validity have been described in the course of considering the quality of measurements. These include construct validity, face validity, predictive validity, concurrent validity, content validity, etc. The descriptions of the different validity types are beyond the scope of this book, but of all the various types of validity, construct validity is the one thought to be all encompassing, and the one we will examine in more detail.

In order to assess construct validity we really need to establish a theoretical background to the measure and to establish what that theory predicts we would see in the measure. But the P scales do not form or represent a tight psychological theoretical construct. They are designed to relate to the National Curriculum which is a well-accepted but, nevertheless, artificial structure. Establishing construct validity in its pure form is not a sensible way to proceed. Instead, we need to look at more prosaic ways of assessing its validity.

Taking another approach, it would be possible to establish validity of the P scales if there was an existing and well-accepted standard method to measure the constructs the P scales are intended to measure.

If we designed a test to measure some property of a subject, for example if we designed a test to measure the ability of a pupil to write, then the test could be subjected to validation by determining the correlation between the results obtained using the test and those obtained by the same pupils using an existing standard test for writing. A high correlation would indicate high validity and vice versa. However, there is no known standard system that measures the attainment levels of pupils working below Level 1 of the National Curriculum. In fact, the most accepted system is the P scales assessment criteria. Therefore it is not possible to conduct a direct validity test on the P scales since there is no existing standard test with which to compare it.

On the other hand, with a large enough dataset one could look at the range of attainments of pupils in the National Curriculum tests and compare them with the results of the P scales to establish whether there is an unbroken continuum between the two. Pupils at the lower end of the national tests should have similar performance levels to those at the top end of the P scales. Further, we can draw on the opinions of experts, teachers and others to ask if, in their opinion, the P scales are fit for purpose.

Demonstrating Reliability and Validity using the P scales

A test system such as the P scales can be (1) reliable but not valid; (2) valid but not reliable; (3) neither reliable nor valid, or (4) both reliable and valid.

1. Consider a pupil whose correct attainment level in Reading is P4. Suppose several teachers assessed her and obtained P7, P7, P8, P7, P8, P8, P7, L1c. These scores are far above P4 but they are very close to each other. Therefore, if it is assumed that the amount of random error associated with the teachers is the same then the assessment system the teachers have used is consistent; that is, the system is reliable. However, the scores are far above the correct attainment level of the pupil, P4. In this case the system has not given correct measurements and is not, therefore,

a valid assessment system although it is reliable because of the similarity of the measurements.

2. Consider a different case where the teachers score the same pupil P2(ii), P3(ii), P4, P4, P5, P6, P6. The scores include the correct attainment level for the child, P4, and other scores fall above and below the correct value. In this case the system is valid because it shows it can measure correctly to a great extent, but unreliable because it is not consistent.

3. Suppose, in another case, the teachers score the pupil P6, P7, L1b, L2b, L3, L5. In this case the scores are widely varied. The system used in the assessment is neither reliable nor valid.

4. Another scenario is that in which the teachers assess the pupil and obtain the following scores P3(ii), P4, P5, P4, P5, P4, P4. In this case the scores are close to an expected score, P4, and are not widely varied. The system used in the assessment is both reliable and valid.

The reliability of data cannot always be attributed to the system or test by which the data was collected. Human beings are susceptible to error. We can be inconsistent as a result of distractions or other causes. Therefore human error will, to a large extent, affect the reliability of data. For example, a case where two teachers assess a pupil in, say, Reading, at the same time, using the same assessment criteria, and award her P3 and P5 respectively, would be attributed not to unreliability of the system, but to differences in the standards applied by the teachers, and an unreliable set of data would be the result.

Reliability and Validity of the P scales Data

The reliability and validity of different methods of assessment are determined by the data collected using those methods.

It was clear that there was a problem in relation to the reliability and validity of the P scales until 2004. There were 14 subjects on which pupils could be assessed on the P scales. If the scales for each of the subjects measured something different then we would expect low to modest correlations between them, i.e correlations in the region of 0.0 to 0.7, but the results from 1999 to 2002 showed that very high correlations existed between the different subject areas.

Table 4.1: Correlation matrix of the cognitive scales for pupils classified as having moderate learning difficulties (MLD). Obtained from 2004 P scales data collected from 1029 schools

	speak.	*listen.*	*read.*	*write.*	*using*	*number*	*shapes*	*sci. enq.*	*life proc.*	*mat. prop.*
speaking										
listening	0.98									
reading	0.86	0.86								
writing	0.87	0.86	0.93							
using	0.80	0.80	0.79	0.81						
number	0.84	0.84	0.85	0.87	0.89					
shape	0.86	0.86	0.85	0.87	0.89	0.93				
sci. enq.	0.78	0.78	0.75	0.78	0.82	0.82	0.83			
life proc.	0.80	0.80	0.76	0.79	0.81	0.82	0.83	0.95		
mat. prop.	0.79	0.79	0.75	0.78	0.82	0.83	0.84	0.96	0.97	
phys. proc	0.78	0.78	0.75	0.78	0.82	0.82	0.84	0.95	0.96	0.97

A typical correlation matrix obtained for all cognitive scales is shown in Table 4.1.

Generally these are high correlations. Similar correlations were obtained in 2001, 2002 and 2003. Further statistical analysis showed that there is only one factor.

Factor analysis of the data generated from the 2001, 2002, 2003 and 2004 P scales indicated the measurement of only one construct. This was also the case in 1999 and 2000. The lowest correlations of 0.75 were obtained between 'Reading' and the Science strands, but that still indicated high similarity between the scales. The scales, though created to measure different constructs were measuring only one. They suggested that the score on one subject could be predicted if the score on another was known.

In 2004 the P scales assessment criteria were reviewed. In 2005 a moderation exercise was conducted by the Qualifications and Curriculum Authority (QCA) to standardise the use of the P scales in pupil assessment.

The correlations for 2006 are shown in Table 4.2.

Table 4.2: Correlation matrix of the cognitive scales for pupils classified as MLD. Obtained from 2006 P scales data collected from 500 schools

	speak.	*listen.*	*read.*	*write.*	*using*	*number*	*shapes*	*sci. enq.*	*life proc.*	*mat. prop.*
speaking										
listening	0.90									
reading	0.65	0.67								
writing	0.65	0.66	0.85							
using	0.67	0.67	0.74	0.75						
number	0.62	0.64	0.79	0.77	0.87					
shape	0.67	0.68	0.76	0.75	0.88	0.89				
sci. enq.	0.64	0.63	0.63	0.64	0.74	0.72	0.75			
life proc.	0.61	0.60	0.64	0.64	0.71	0.72	0.75	0.92		
mat. prop.	0.63	0.62	0.65	0.65	0.72	0.72	0.76	0.94	0.95	
phys. proc	0.62	0.61	0.64	0.64	0.71	0.72	0.76	0.93	0.96	0.97

It is obvious from the correlation matrix of the 2006 data, Table 4.2, that the correlations between 'Speaking' and 'Listening' and the other strands, especially 'Reading' and 'Writing', were lower than in the 2004 data. The correlations between 'Speaking' and 'Listening' and the strands of Mathematics and Science were all lower than they were in 2004, as was the correlation between Mathematics and Science. Factor analysis found two factors. The English and Mathematics strands constituted one factor and the Science strands another. The 2006 P scales measured two attributes, where they had measured only one up to 2004.

The correlation matrices of 2006/2007 demonstrate clearly the improvement in the quality of the P scales data after the review of the criteria and the moderation exercise.

Similar correlations were obtained in 2007 as shown in Table 4.3.

There are two possible reasons why the different strands of the P scales could have been measuring one attribute. It could have been the result of similarities between the level descriptors of the different strands, for example if the level descriptors of, say, P4, P5, P6, P7, and P8, etc., in one strand or subject area are similar to the

Table 4.3: Correlation matrix of the cognitive scales for pupils classified as MLD. Obtained from 2007 P scales data collected from 528 schools

	speak.	*listen.*	*read.*	*write.*	*using*	*number*	*shapes*	*sci. enq*	*life proc.*	*mat. prop.*
speaking										
listening	0.88									
reading	0.62	0.66								
writing	0.62	0.63	0.84							
using	0.66	0.67	0.75	0.74						
number	0.64	0.65	0.79	0.78	0.86					
shape	0.67	0.67	0.75	0.75	0.89	0.87				
sci. enq	0.63	0.63	0.61	0.63	0.73	0.71	0.73			
life proc.	0.60	0.60	0.61	0.64	0.71	0.71	0.74	0.94		
mat. prop	0.62	0.61	0.62	0.64	0.72	0.72	0.74	0.95	0.96	
phys proc	0.62	0.61	0.61	0.63	0.71	0.70	0.73	0.93	0.96	0.96

descriptors of the corresponding levels in other strands, then high correlations would be expected between those strands. Human error could also result in high correlations between the strands.

Analysis of the P scales to examine whether there were incidents of pupils scoring the same levels in many or all of the strands was carried out by isolating those pupils who scored the same P level in all subject strands. This showed that, out of more than 22,000 pupils in the 2006 P scales data, about half scored the same P level in all subjects. It would seem that once a pupil is seen as a 'P4 child' or a 'P7 child' in, say, 'Speaking', the child could be allocated the same level in all subjects without proper assessment. This gives rise to the so-called 'halo' effect in the data.

Do the Curriculum Areas of the P scales Discriminate?

A good assessment system should be able to discriminate between high and low performing pupils. It should also discriminate between different levels in each curriculum area. Do the P scales discriminate between low and high achievers? Do they discriminate between levels on the scale?

In order to answer these questions the dataset of attainment scores of pupils assessed in 2006 was analysed using the Item Response Theory (IRT). Earlier analysis had shown similar characteristics between datasets collected each year since 1999. Therefore, it did not matter which dataset was used for the analysis. For example, there were no great differences in the correlations between subject areas over the years. Analysis of the 2005 and 2006 datasets by IRT showed no marked differences.

Results of the IRT analysis showed that the P scales can discriminate between high and low achievers. They also showed that they can discriminate between levels on the scale. It was found that 'Listening' and all the strands of Mathematics and Science discriminate between high and low performing pupils more than expected for items of similar difficulty.

In summary, this chapter has discussed the meanings of validity and reliability as they apply to the P scales. It has shown how to conduct reliability and validity tests on the P scales and has demonstrated that teacher reliability can be assessed at school and LA levels with resulting improvements. It has covered the review of the P scales in 2004 and the moderation exercise conducted by the QCA, which together have improved the quality of the data collected.

Finally we have seen that the P scales can discriminate between high and low performing pupils and between the levels in each scale, both of the greatest importance for a successful assessment system.

Further Reading

Masters GN (1988) Item discrimination: When more is worse, *Journal of Educational Measurement*, 25(1), 15.

Zumbo BD (1999) *A Handbook on the Theory and Methods of Differential Item Functioning (DIF)*. Ottawa: Directorate of Human Research and Evaluation, National Defence Headquarters.

www.winsteps.com

CHAPTER 5

Users' Perspectives

Celia Dickinson, Bob Coburn,
Helen Pettinger, John Parkes, Ginny Brown,
Di Brown, Bernie Tetchner, Jo Gilbert and Mary Adossides

As the title implies, this chapter consists of contributions from nine teachers from eight different special schools. Essentially, these are accounts of their use of the P scales in their respective schools as a tool for assessment of pupils' attainment and progress as well as general school improvement.

Celia Dickinson – Cavendish School, Runcorn, Cheshire

When asked to write a contribution to this book on Cavendish School's experience and use of P scales my first reaction was, where do I begin? P scales have been a pivotal tool in the school's development of assessment for learning over 10 years so I therefore propose I take you on our learning journey over that period of time.

Firstly, I take this opportunity to put the school in context, giving you an overview of where we were in 1997 to where we are today in 2007. Cavendish School was, until 2006, designated a school for pupils aged 2–19 with profound and severe learning difficulties. In 2006 we were re-designated as a school for pupils aged 11–19 with

The P scales: Assessing the Progress of Children with Special Educational Needs
Written and edited by Francis Ndaji and Peter Tymms
Copyright © 2009 John Wiley & Sons Ltd.

profound and multiple learning difficulties (PMLD), severe learning difficulties (SLD) and autistic spectrum disorder (ASD). The
school has also seen an increased intake of pupils who have moderate learning difficulties (MLD) with additional emotional vulnerability (BESD). All pupils have a statement of Special Educational
Need; occasionally the school will undertake the full diagnostic
assessment as part of the Halton Borough's statementing procedures, STAMP. The statementing procedures in Halton remain a
holistic assessment process with an emphasis on diagnostic assessment, principally through educational psychology testing.

The school has always embraced Government initiatives, in particular, in its early adoption of the National Curriculum in 1988. Like
many special schools at this time the school re-wrote its teaching
and learning policies, moving from a medical or behavioural curriculum to a subject specific curriculum; that is, Language and Communication to English: 'Speaking and Listening'; Money and
Shopping to Mathematics: 'Using and applying'; and so on. This was
the beginning of putting structure into the curriculum, and learning
opportunities opened up that previously had been hidden within
developmental criteria for learning. As a natural progression the
school therefore looked at its assessment procedures. We used
several medically driven diagnostic tests including auditory, visual,
language and behavioural criteria. As staff became more skilled in
planning teaching through the National Curriculum they felt they
needed more precision in our assessment, which would be agreed
and transferable from class to class. Furthermore, this had now
become a matter of equal opportunity for our pupils and a passion
to celebrate their achievements within an inclusive education system.

'W' (working towards Level 1 of the National Curriculum) is
disheartening and did not reflect the significant achievement our
pupils made within National Curriculum subjects and so in 1991/2
we devised our own assessment procedures using a piece of developmental software known as The Annual Review System, which
was produced by what is now known as SEMERC. Although it was
a little known system, it enabled us to systematically assess our
pupils against an internally agreed criterion. The system produced
individual reports with 'stepping-stones' achievement, a 'can do'
assessment removing any outcomes that had not been achieved.
Obviously those stepping-stones not yet achieved could become the
foundation of target-setting for future curriculum planning. Again,

from a senior leadership point of view the system produced analysis of pupil learning including rankings, which could be used in monitoring whole-school progress in English, Mathematics, Science and PSHE.

In 1997, the school was asked to pilot assessment work by NfER commissioned by SCAA (QCA), which eventually became P scales/ P-Levels (2000). The staff immediately felt they could work with the assessment criteria and without question the teachers baseline assessed all pupils. The pilot studies and outcomes have been covered in other sections; however, the school has faced a number of difficulties such as assessment of current level, not achieved level, teaching to the P-Level, etc. The latter is still particularly prevalent with newly qualified teachers. All pupils were assessed. This included nursery-aged children and post-16 years, although the school no longer assesses this age group in line with QCA guidance.

Today, the school uses P-Level assessment at three different levels:

1. Whole school data analysis to support school improvement target setting.
2. Tracking cohort and individual pupil progress over a Key Stage.
3. Assessment to inform individual target setting and teacher differentiation in planning.

Whole school data

The school uses the data from the CEM at Durham University to inform our self-review processes as demonstrated in the model below:

As a school leader, the information provided by the CEM enables me to analyse (1) whole school strengths and weaknesses; (2) comparative data with other schools within the project; and (3) value added data.

The graphs are particularly useful in giving an instant overall picture of attainment against the P-Levels. How does this work in practice? Figure 5.2 gives a copy of Cavendish School's data in Mathematics.

Figures 5.2(a) and 5.2(b) are described in greater detail in Chapter 6.

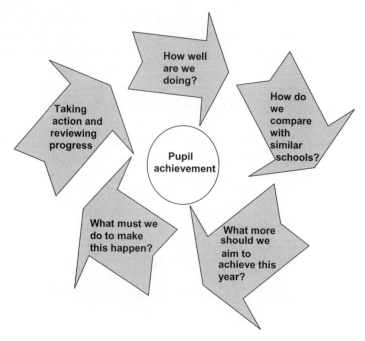

Figure 5.1: A self-review model adopted by Cavendish School.

How well are we doing?

The results, although good, demonstrate greater achievement in 'Number' than in 'Using and applying'. An audit trail of teacher planning, timetable balance and pupil records of achievement revealed that teachers focused mainly on 'Number' including number recognition and calculation. There was less emphasis on applying these skills in a wider forum and on practical tasks due to a traditional approach to teaching using worksheets and rote counting.

How do we compare with similar schools?

Overall we compare well. In both areas we are within or above the Interquartile Range. We are making good progress at Year 5 and maintaining good progress at Year Groups 10, 11 and 12.

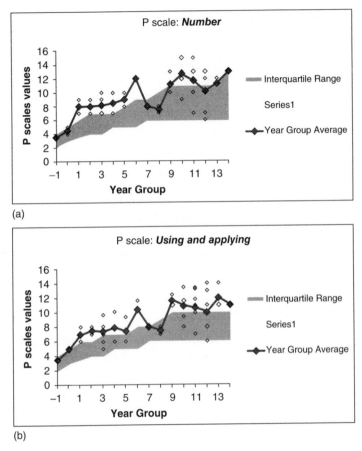

Figure 5.2: (a): Results for Number. **(b):** Results for 'Using and applying'.

What more should we aim to achieve next year?

A whole school target was set to improve our results in Mathematics: 'Using and applying'. Individual pupil targets were set using P-level results that ranged from significant progress within a P-level to a full P scale improvement. Through analysis of individual P-level targeting, a whole-school target of 80% of pupils assessed at P4 and above will make a full P-level improvement over a two-year period.

What must we do to make this happen?

The results outlined above were for 2003/04 and we reassessed the way we teach. The school changed its pedagogy and focused on the way children learn. Staff developed a deeper understanding of kinaesthetic learning, which was particularly successful in raising standards in the practical mathematics of using and applying number.

Taking action and reviewing progress

Teachers focused on pupil learning including the way children learn. Pupil progress was tracked each half term and learning outcomes evaluated regularly.

The following year's results in Mathematics are shown in Figure 5.3.

Tracking pupil attainment

Using P scales to track pupil attainment is a contentious area. P scales are a summative assessment over a Key Stage.

'The level descriptors provide the basis for making judgement in pupils' performance at the end of Key Stages 1, 2 & 3' QCA Guidance: Performance – P Level attainment targets (QCA, 2007).

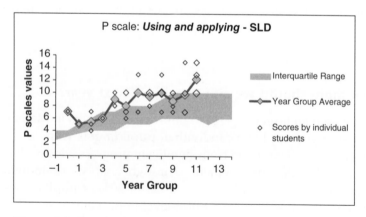

Figure 5.3: Results for 'Using and applying' for the next year.

In reality schools are required to demonstrate pupil progress annually and at Cavendish School we assess pupil attainment each year. The school uses a commercially produced package that provides statistical analysis of pupil attainment in a variety of ways, including:

1. individual pupil profile
2. individual pupil performance
3. subject profile
4. pupil ranking
5. pupil summary
6. percentage movement
7. values percentiles
8. audit trail.

The package subdivides the P-level into five 'Performance Indicators' that have value scores. It is through these subdivisions that school leaders and teachers can demonstrate progress on an annual basis.

Individual pupil target setting and planning for differentiation

QCA Guidance (QCA, 2007) states that:

> 'The performance descriptors should be used by teachers in the same way as the main National Curriculum Level Descriptors. In deciding on a pupil level of attainment at the end of a Key Stage, teachers should judge which descriptor best fits pupils performance.'

The descriptions in the subject materials can be used by staff in the same way as the National Curriculum level descriptions to:

- develop or support more focused day-to-day approaches to ongoing teacher assessment by using the descriptions to refine and develop long-, medium- and short-term planning
- track linear progress towards subject-specific attainment at National Curriculum Level 1
- identify lateral progress by looking for related skills at similar levels across subjects

- record pupils' overall development and achievement, for example, at the end of a year or a Key Stage
- decide which description best fits a pupil's performance over a period of time and in different contexts, using their (teachers') professional judgement.

Without doubt at Cavendish School, teachers effectively use teacher assessment to inform planning. Our planning is minimalist due to the linkage between assessment and evaluation of learning outcomes. Long-term planning is based on National Curriculum Guidance and we have 2-year, 3-year and 4-year programmes depending on Key Stage. There are no fixed schemes of work! We use assessment to judge the programmes of study the Key Stage cohorts will access. To describe best how this works is, perhaps, to look at Shakespeare. National Curriculum Guidance for English recommends that pupils study at least one piece of Shakespeare at Key Stage 4. We could say that at Key Stage 4 all pupils will study *Macbeth*, this could be because the current recommendation for GCSE English that year is Macbeth so we are inclusive in our studies. Or, we could look at the P-Level results of the cohort and judge which of Shakespeare's works would be more appropriate to their level of learning. We have had a cohort of Key Stage 4 pupils who were overall P8 – NC Level 3. For this cohort it was decided to study *A Midsummer's Night Dream*: one of the more complicated of Shakespearian plays with three stories in one. I confess I thought this something of a challenge, but as always, my staff rose to this. Over the 12-month period of study the pupils excelled themselves in understanding the play, which was evident in their P-Level English results but even more in their PHSEC&C results. It was wonderful. The current cohort of Key Stage 4 pupils' results is circa P4-P8 with equivalent PHSEC&C. For this cohort it has been decided to study *Romeo and Juliet*, which was judged to be more appropriate to the pupils' level of learning.

The teachers complete one planning set per subject, per term as shown in Table 5.1. The planning is focused on the learning outcomes, using the subjects as a vehicle for learning. The right column indicates the desirable learning outcomes across the learning spectrum of the class. The assessed level of learning of individual pupils

Table 5.1: Teacher's planning sheet for Number

PLANNING: SENIOR 1
Subject: Mathematics/Numeracy
Area of Study: Number – Addition and Subtraction

Handling Data – dates of birth

Date	Lesson plan	Learning outcomes
9.3.07	Composition of dates 1990s Year 2000 Counting in tens	Pupils to participate/learn rote counting to 10. Pupils to participate/learn rote counting in 10s.
16.3.07	Rote counting 1–9 Years 1970, 1971, 1972, etc., to 1990 Pupils' birth years	Pupils to know and understand place value of 10 in calendar calculation. Pupils to know and understand number of months in a year and days in a week.
23.3.07	Days of the week Counting to 30 Day number representation in dates Pupils to write DoB. in numeric format	Pupils to know and understand that dates can written in numeric form.
30.3.07	Revisit weeks previous half-term Pupils recognise date of birth in numeric format Form filling	Pupils to know own birth date in numeric form. Pupils to be able to complete date of birth area of form in numeric form.
6.4.07	Mental calculation games on ages using dates of birth: add on and subtraction	Pupils to recognise relationship between date of birth and year ages.
13.4.07	Date compositions – assessment	Pupils to learn calculation of time and dates.

determines the learning outcomes. Individual learning targets for pupils are then transferred to their Individual Educational Plan, which is linked to their P-Level assessment and specific learning need as described in Table 5.2.

The planning and recording process is ultimately used to make teacher judgement on pupil progress and to assess the P-Level. It is

Table 5.2 Individual learning targets for pupils (pseudonyms used).

Pupil name	Individual learning target	Learning outcome	P-Level
James Dogood	James to rote count to 12. James to know own birth date in numeric form James to know number of months in a year	James was unable to rote count beyond four independently James joined in the date game and was able to recognise his own birth date on the board. However unable to generalise this activity	P6
Sarah Tringa	Sarah to know and understand number of months in a year and days in a week Sarah to know and understand dates can be written in numeric form Sarah to know own birth date in numeric form Sarah to be able to complete date of birth area of form in numeric form Sarah to recognise relationship between date of birth and year ages	Sarah achieved 1, 2, 3, 4 of her targets within the group sessions The targets require generalising into 'official' forms, etc The calculation for five was beyond her understanding, however, there was a gap in lesson continuity	2B
Banners Colkey	Banners to participate in rote counting to 10 Banners to participate in rote counting in 10s To know two number songs for 10	Banners participated in the songs through clapping and singing Banners followed by eye pointing the counting sessions although did not understand the concept of number	P4
Chinchin Bingham	Chinchin to be able to complete date of birth area of form in numeric form Chinchin to recognise relationship between date of birth and year ages Chinchin to learn calculation of time and dates	Chinchin has good grasp of dates in numeric form Chinchin knows that the year indicates age and was able to calculate his and others' ages through rote calculation	P8

Name	Objectives	Outcomes	
Michael Forth	Michael to know and understand number of months in a year and days in a week Michael to know and understand dates can be written in numeric form Michael to know own birth date in numeric form Michael to be able to complete date of birth area of form in numeric form	Michael was beginning to understand that the date could be written in numeric form, however was easily confused when confronted with the day's date written in full Michael recognised his own and most other birth dates on the board game Michael knows there are 12 months in a year and that each month can be represented by a number Michael will need to generalise his skills and became confused when the continuity of lessons was disrupted	P7
Tina Pennyson	Tina to know and understand number of months in a year and days in a week	Tina participated in the group activities and was able to indicate her own birth date on board game	P5
Nick Kings	Nick to know and understand number of months in a year and days in a week Nick to know and understand dates can written in numeric form Nick to know own birth date in numeric form Nick to be able to complete date of birth area of form in numeric form	Nick recognises his own birth date in numeric form on board game Nick recognises how to write birth date in numeric form and is beginning to do this unaided	P7
Zara Manilup	Zara to know and understand number of months in year and days in a week Zara to know and understand dates can be written in numeric form Zara to know own birth date in numeric form Zara to be able to complete date of birth area of form in numeric form	Zara understands the months of the year and that they can be written in numeric form Prompted, Zara is able to write his own birth date and the day's date in numeric form, however he always uses reversals!	P6

evident by the process that assessment is a continuous process. At the end of the academic year the school undertakes a formal assessment using P-Levels criteria, which is used for data collection by the DCSF and, for our own purposes, Durham University.

One issue raised in assessment is the dependency on teacher judgement. As assessment for learning is fundamental to the way in which we work at Cavendish School, time is made available to all teachers to complete our assessment processes. This includes two days in June for teachers to complete end-of-year summative assessment. Department/Key Stage teachers work collaboratively to assess pupil work in English, Mathematics, Science and PHSEC&C, jointly making judgement on the final summative P-Level assessment. Comment on how the judgement was reached, supported by examples of pupil work, is completed and kept in the pupils' Record of Achievement files. The school's 2005 OfSTED Inspection Report states:

> 'Assessment is Excellent, and, because of this, teachers have a very good knowledge of the learning needs and capabilities of those they teach.'

The School Improvement Cycle poses the question of how well we achieve compared to others. The school values the comparative data provided through the CEM at Durham University in supporting professional dialogue to drive forward school improvement. The school is not in competition with other schools, indeed the data does not list comparative schools. However, the overview of where the school sits in terms of like learners is helpful in whole school target setting. An example would be our current PHSEC&C results, which, compared to other years, are not as high achieving. The school has always prided itself in its high achievements in PHSEC&C. The fall is at Years 7 and 8, getting back on track by Year 11. Furthermore, our 'Speaking/Listening' results are not as high as in previous years. The analysis leads us to see linkage between the two subjects in terms of confident citizens, which, in turn, reflects the changing nature of our pupil intake. The impact of emotional vulnerability on the pupils' learning at ages 11–13 is immense and is a whole school issue across all areas of the curriculum.

The school currently receives value-added data from the CEM at Durham University, which is challenging our thinking. Returning to our current results for mathematics, our comparative data indicates we are achieving well and above the interquartile range. However, the value-added results for 2005–2006 demonstrate that pupils are achieving within expectation, only 8% of pupils are in the top 16% in English with 14% in the bottom 16%; in Mathematics 5% in the top 2.5%, 8% in the top 16%, 5% in the bottom 16% and 2% in the bottom 2.5%; in Science 6% in the top 2.5%, 20% in the top 16% and 5% in the bottom 16%. These results bring us back full circle in professional dialogue. The questions posed include:

- are we teaching to the P-Level?
- how do we moderate the assessment?
- should we concern ourselves on annual assessment?
- what will the value-added results be over a Key Stage?
- does it really matter?

If pupils are doing as well as expected, with some doing a bit better – a leap of learning, we call it at Cavendish School – and with some, unfortunately, for now, not leaping as well as we thought they would that year, does it really matter? Our journey has brought us to look at learning in depth. We are awaiting the next two years' value-added data before we can judge pupil learning through this data. However, we believe the impact the data collection and participation in the Durham research project over the years has had on our approach to learning is invaluable. We have moved on in teaching and learning, embracing Mind-based / Accelerated learning and adopting a child-centred approach to learning. To that end the school is working with the European Agency for Special Needs Education and QCA in looking at developing pupil learning passports and self-assessment. We are using Thinking Skills and Thinking Maps as a way of tracking learning. It is hoped that by combining Thinking Maps as formative assessment and P-Levels as summative assessment we will achieve a true picture of pupil learning and attainment. The best judge of attainment is by the pupils themselves, this is our ultimate goal and we look forward to using all data to improve their learning.

Bob Coburn – Curnow School, Redruth, Cornwall

The context

This contribution will describe the journey Curnow School has taken over the past two years (to January 2008) as it has moved from a special school that was failing to one that is making significant improvements. Central to the progress of the school has been the emphasis placed on the creation and use of good and robust data. In turn, key to this has been the developing use of the P scales.

In January 2006, Curnow School was a troubled school. Confused leadership and poorly thought-through managerial decisions had resulted in a great number of difficulties. Although this had not been confirmed through inspection, the local authority regarded it at that time as a school that was failing its 115 pupils with severe learning difficulties. It was suffering from acute budgetary problems, inadequate curriculum organisation, poor teaching and learning, and confused data.

The Assistant Headteacher was working very hard to manage the P scales data within the school, but because of the lack of clear leadership and direction this effort was not being effective. The collection process was unclear; the relationship between the current year's assessments and previous years' was poor, and, once collected and collated, the data were then put on a shelf and forgotten until the next year. The P scales data were not seen as means to improve understanding of the children's learning and, therefore, to improve teaching, but as an administrative task that was entirely separate. The data ran parallel to teaching and learning.

We did have two advantages, however. We had been part of the Durham University P scales project since its inception, and we had a fabulous Statistics Department in Cornwall who were very keen to learn and help. We had all the means whereby we could analyse the data: the problem was that the data we were producing were not up to the job.

How we tackled the problem

To address the issues of P scales data within the school, a sub-group of the Governors was set up along with the newly appointed

Headteacher, Assistant Headteacher and LA Inspector. This group identified that there were two sorts of issues: general issues with using P scales data in a special school, and issues specific to Curnow School.

General issues

The group felt that the data, while apparently interesting, must always be approached with some caution as the sizes of the cohorts are so small. This potentially produces great volatility in the final 'scores' as a single child's progress can have a significant impact on the final result.

Similarly, the P scales reflect 'vertical' progress: movement up (or down) the scales. They do not necessarily reflect 'lateral' progress such as when a child develops greater understanding within a scale but does not actually cross the (sometimes arbitrary) border between one scale and another. With pupils classified as having Profound and Multiple Learning Difficulties (PMLD) for example, who may take a very long time to move from one scale to another, this must not be interpreted that they have not made any progress. For a number of learners, lateral progress is at least as significant as vertical progress: unfortunately it is much more difficult to capture and record.

The final general issue concerns the status of the P scales data. While they appear to be objective because they are written in the form of numbers, they are in fact highly subjective as they are the 'best fit' within a range of possible measures. They are 'qualitative' measures presented in a 'quantitative' form. This is both their advantage and their disadvantage. While it prevents the scales being overly prescriptive it also means that, by being subjective, they are at the mercy of different teachers' interpretations and the general context in which they were produced. For example, it became clear during analysis of the data at the school that, in a previous year, one teacher had consistently 'over-graded' her children, presumably to provide 'evidence' that she was a 'good teacher'. In subsequent years, a more realistic grading meant that the children's learning may have appeared to have stalled or even regressed when in fact they had continued to make steady progress.

Curnow School issues

There were a number of examples at Curnow School of this inconsistent collecting, recording and moderating of the P scales. As such, the sub-group confirmed that the data from previous years were flaky and needed to be approached with caution.

Similarly, there was no system for analysing the data by particular cohorts within the school. For example, no analysis was made of any differences based on gender, looked after children, need type, or by class or year group.

Finally, as noted above, the data were not used to inform future planning nor were they incorporated into the strategic planning of the school.

What we needed to do

From our analysis, the sub-group realised that to improve standards at the school, we needed to ensure that:

- the data collected were an accurate reflection of the children's level of understanding
- the levels recorded were consistent across the school
- the data were collected in an efficient and effective manner, and based on current and prior attainment
- the data were capable of being disentangled to reflect the progress and attainment of different sub-groups within the school
- the data were analysed in depth to inform:
  - strategic planning
  - planning for class activities
  - planning for personalised learning
- through the analysis of the data, succinct reporting could be made that could then be used within the self-evaluation form (SEF)
- a system was developed that recognised 'lateral' learning within a P scale as well as 'vertical' learning from one P scale to another
- the data were analysed on an individual class basis and informed the setting of Pupil Progress Targets for Teachers' Performance Management.

What we actually did

Once the sub-group had considered the data process at the school, a number of actions were immediately put into place.

Assessment Cycle

Firstly, we developed an Assessment Cycle in the school and incorporated it into the School Self-Evaluation Policy and Guidelines (SSEPG). This made explicit exactly when the data were to be produced and how and when they were to be analysed. It also allowed us to concentrate on different aspects of the P scales and their use within the school.

Moderation

It is important that there is consistency of recording progress within the P scales to ensure that the quantitative measures are an accurate reflection of the qualitative judgements. To this end, over the academic year nine teachers' meetings (three per term) are dedicated to the moderation of the P scales to ensure there is consistency. Examples of specified levels (e.g. P4 'Speaking') are brought to the meeting and discussed by the whole teaching staff. Not only does this help staff in their own judgements, but it has the added spin-off of enabling staff to look at the P scales of children other than those in their class. This has helped them recognise the variety of needs within the school and the range of responses that constitute a similar level.

Data analysis

A 'Data Day' takes place in the autumn term of each year where the Teaching, Learning and Assessment Sub Committee of the Governors meet with the Leadership Team and the LA Inspector to interrogate the data. For this the Leadership Team are released from classroom duties for the whole day. The Data Day takes into account national data (through the Durham Project); local data produced by the Statistics Team; and the specific school data. The aim is to interrogate the P scales data to know how well we are performing against similar schools nationally and locally, as well as clearly identifying where improvements can be made to our own practice. Once analysed, an Action Plan is produced that is then put into place. For example, the data may suggest that the children have not made the same progress in 'Shape, space and measures' that they have done in 'Number'. Therefore, the school should focus on this in a number of ways: for example, bringing forward the planned evaluation of the Mathematics teaching in the school and focusing this upon 'Shape, space and measures' while also commissioning advice and input from the Mathematics Advisor.

Different cohorts

At the first meeting of the sub-group, through the LA Inspector, a data analysis system was commissioned from the Statistic Team of the Local Authority, based on the already excellent system provided. The team worked diligently on this and it was ready for the Data Day in November 2007. This proved to be a powerful tool for it not only enabled us to interrogate the data in many different forms so that smaller sub-groups within the school can be recognised and targeted, but, by being 'projectable' through a laptop and projector, it also allowed us to easily see the results as we moved from one analysis to another. The system had the added bonus of automatically producing pie charts of the different cohorts as they were actively constructed. The data, once analysed, enabled the school to succinctly report within the SEF the pupils' and students' progress and attainment.

> Curnow School SEF: Section 3a – What are the learners' achievements and standards in their work?

> Analysis of the 2006-7 P scales data shows that standards for those learners within Lower and Middle Faculties compare positively against national data for special schools produced by Durham University and against local data produced by the LA. At the end of KS2 and KS3, progress made by the majority of the learners was greater than that of other similar schools within the LA. While the KS1 progress compared favourably against local levels, it was felt that this was not a complete reflection of the progress made by the pupils. A change in teachers within this group was made as a result and will be monitored during the 2007-8 academic year. The progress

made by the KS4 students was below that of the 2006-7 data. Analysis of the uncorroborated data on KS4 progression in May/June 2007 enabled the school to review its KS4 curriculum and staffing and, as a result of this, implement a revised KS4 curriculum from September 2007. This will be evaluated in July 2008 as part of the School Improvement Plan (SIP). In November 2007, Governors, the Leadership Team and the LA Inspector interrogated the P scale data for different sub-groups within the school. Key points were: 1) evidence of a steady increase in numbers of pupils progressing one unit on the P scales; 2) evidence of reduced numbers of pupils regressing one unit on the P scales; 3) the underperformance of KS4 identified above was confirmed (plan already put into place): 4) above average progress for learners who are Looked After. This interrogation of the data also revealed that there had been an improvement in the security of the judgements based upon 2005-6, which in turn had been more secure than 2004-5. The introduction of B-squared (an assessment system developed from the P scales) in October 2007 will impact further on this. There has been a 100% increase (from 0%–100%) in the number of students achieving accreditation in Accreditation in Living and Learning (an externally accredited course specifically for students with severe learning difficulties) in Post 16 during the 2006-7 academic year.

At the Data Day held in November 2007, the system not only allowed us to look at the data for the whole school but it also facilitated the analysis of the progress and attainment of different sub-groups within the school. The sub-group were able to look at the data broken down by:

- gender
- looked after children
- ethnicity
- need types (e.g. PMLD, ASD)
- year groups.

In all, we were able to analyse the data from 26 different sub-groups within the school. Amongst the many conclusions reached, it identified that the looked after children made greater progress than other groups within the school, therefore providing evidence that targeted input, as is required for looked after children, does indeed have an impact. Similarly, by breaking down the data into year groups, we were able to confirm the earlier conclusion that the Key Stage 4 group had not made the progress hoped for, and it allowed for monitoring and evaluation of the new curriculum package put into place for the 2007–8 academic year.

Lateral Progress

To accurately record progress made within the individual P scales, it was decided to use the electronic assessment system, B squared. By breaking down the P scales into component parts, this allowed us to identify where progress had taken place and how much. We could, therefore, identify with greater accuracy when a child has moved from 'just starting' on a P level to one where they have almost completed it. We were able to identify the children in the classes who were close to fully achieving the P scales level so that they could be targeted, thereby moving them towards the next level on the P scales.

B squared was installed on our internal network, and in October 2007, all teaching staff received training plus release time to update for all the learners in their classes. This is now being used to produce P scales data for each Annual Review and to inform Individual Education Plans as appropriate.

Assessment weeks are built into the school Assessment Cycle, where the focus of the week is on identifying exactly where each child is on the different P scales. The B squared records are formally updated during these weeks, bringing together the assessments at other times.

Strategic planning

The rigorous scrutiny of the data enabled the Leadership and Governors to make informed decisions over the strategic planning for the school. For example, the underperformance of Key Stage 4 pupils in the 2006–2007 year resulted in a change in staffing plus a complete reorganisation of the curriculum structure and means of delivery. While this is still to be confirmed through data analysis, early indications are that this has been successful and progress and attainment have improved. Similarly, while pupils' progress in Key Stage 1 in 2006–2007 was within national and local averages, we felt that this did not fully reflect the children's actual levels of attainment and that there had been some issues in the accuracy of the data. The teachers were changed in the classes, and again this is being carefully monitored.

Teacher development

Each teacher is given the P scales data for each of the children in their class. This identifies in both numeric and graphic form the current attainment of the children, plus a record of their progress over the past five years. While, as noted above, it should be remembered that the data pre-2006 is not reliable, it still does give a useful indication of how the children are progressing. Progress and attainment in English, Maths, Science, PSHE/C and ICT are recorded. The teachers then use this information in their day-to-day planning, both for the class and for individual learning.

Furthermore, the teachers use the P scales data for the children in their class to inform the identification of the Pupil Progress Target for their own Performance Management. This has been very beneficial and helped focus the discussion. For example, one teacher identified that two children in her class had lower levels of attainment in 'Speaking' and 'Listening' than did other pupils. Starting from this point, we speculated over why this could be occurring and we identified that both children had a hearing loss. One possibility was that the use of Makaton was not consistent between members of staff and this may have been inhibiting language development. The target then became one where the teacher worked on her Makaton skills, and ran sessions on Makaton with the Learning Support Assistants in the class. Similarly, with another teacher we identified that three of his pupils were all very close to completing a P scales target in PSHE/C, and that a specific focus on this for a term would be able to raise their attainment and therefore take them to the next P scale. In this way, individual teacher development is tied explicitly to the overall strategic development of the school.

To move a failing school to a successful one is a complex operation and it needs to be done with determined care and diligence. It is too easy to 'blame' a lack of progress on the children's significant learning difficulties rather than on what we are doing with them. To know when progress has taken place and to identify the best ways forward, good data are essential. By this close relationship with data, Curnow School has moved from the position of a failing school in January 2006 to one that was judged Satisfactory by Ofsted in June 2007. We still have a long way to go, but P scales data are going to be constant companions on our journey.

Helen Pettinger – Mountjoy Special School, Bridport, Dorset

The P scales have been in use in special schools for many years, but have not been widely used in mainstream schools because the majority of children with Special Educational Needs were either placed in special schools or residential units where specialist services were available. That was until local authorities began driving an 'Inclusion for All' approach that saw a dramatic turn-around in the number of youngsters being 'integrated' into mainstream establishments. The inclusion approach resulted in many children with complex learning needs, physical disabilities, sensory impairments, autistic spectrum disorders, and visual and hearing impairments attending mainstream schools. Teaching staff were expected at the end of the academic year or Key Stage to be able to demonstrate how all their pupils (including those with Special Educational Needs) performed and the P scales provided a means to accomplish this task for those pupils with Special Educational Needs who work below Level 1 of the National Curriculum. Despite the government's 'Inclusion for All' approach the majority of pupils with SEN are still placed in special schools where the P scales are the tool for assessing pupils' attainments and progress.

In assessment, teachers have always been expected to show how their pupils make progress. Where the individual pupil has been assessed as working below the National Curriculum they have, until recently been expected to report a 'W' but the emphasis is now on a score using the P-levels. In time this will be a national expectation and comparisons nationally will be made in the same way standard data are presented.

This case study is based on direct experience and will examine the strengths and the drawbacks associated with using the P scales in different situations.

A newly-qualified teacher working in an inner-city primary school was faced with a complex class of 30 Year One children;

17 of whom had Special Educational Needs of varying types. The staff in this class consisted of an inexperienced teacher and a teaching assistant. The majority of these children on the special needs register were achieving below the National Curriculum level and it was problematic demonstrating that they were making progress. Through discussion with experienced colleagues from other schools, this teacher realised that the P scales might be a useful tool, so she set about assessing these children with the P-level criteria and these pupils were shown to make progress through the criterion. However, in hindsight, it was obvious that this was done very naively and, as the case study will explore, the assessments should not have been made as a one-off judgement on one piece of work, they would have to become integral to the teaching and assessment that continued throughout the year; but it was a start and it demonstrated that those 'under-achieving' pupils made significant progress.

Knowledge of the P scales and the use of them have spread widely and teaching colleagues in both mainstream and specialist environments use the P-level criteria to make professional judgements on the pupils they are working with. As with any assessment tool there are drawbacks alongside the positive elements of using the P scales. These will be explored next with evidence how the P scales have been used and experienced in different situations.

In one local authority, an Assessment forum was initiated and a selected group of practitioners who were familiar with the P-levels were asked to work on developing a moderation pack to support teachers in using the levels and to start looking at some of the drawbacks. This group consisted of both mainstream and special school teachers, Headteachers and Local Authority Inspectors.

There was a general concern about when the P-levels should begin to be used to support teacher judgements. Obviously, in mainstream settings, children in the Early Years would be following the Foundation Stage Curriculum and should be working towards this assessment criteria. However, there are a number of children who do not demonstrate progress in some areas of the Foundation Stage. Often it is thought that P scales could be used at this point to show that this small cohort of children are continuing to make progress albeit at a slower rate in comparison to other pupils.

There were situations when the group deemed it necessary to use the P-levels at such an early stage. This would be usually in a specialist provision where the pupil has not made progress in early development, possibly with physical or sensory impairments. There was a definite agreement between group members that in normal circumstances the P-levels should not be used until the second term in Year One (National Curriculum). This was to allow the youngest pupils to develop in maturity and independence. This also gave these children opportunities to succeed at the Foundation Stage objectives before deeming them to have Special Educational Needs.

The next step was to plan the moderation pack and try to envisage what this would look like. It had to be user-friendly and informative to ensure that practitioners could use this confidently to support their judgements using the P scales. The group decided that they would focus on 'Writing' initially and they set about agreement trialling on packs of work from pupils. One difficulty with this exercise was that there appeared to be little work at P4 or below and it was agreed that the moderation pack would support P4–P8, which proved to be a very useful tool for the majority of mainstream colleagues, but for those teachers who had pupils functioning below P4 there was still no supporting evidence to aid their professional judgements.

The lower P-levels relied on the professionalism of the teachers working with this small number of youngsters and the moderation processes set up in the individual schools. Due to the complex difficulties the pupils functioning at these lower levels would display, the only evidence would be video and photographic, which is often left open to interpretation as this evidence does not always display the amount of support given or the context in which it is being assessed. The moderation process at this level therefore is far more problematic and relies solely on the teacher's knowledge of the pupil. Obviously the majority of children functioning at this level will already be in specialist establishments and so opportunities for collaboration across the special schools would be advantageous.

Questions arose throughout this project which had to be solved before the moderation pack could be developed further.

Could an assessment be made solely on the evidence of work at this level?

Discussion grew around the quality of the work, especially looking at the lower end of the P-levels P4 and P5 which demonstrate emerging skills in many areas. The group found that knowing the child as an individual supported any assessment. Other factors were considered when making a judgement, for example, the rate of progress, the learning styles, the specific difficulties and the area of needs had to be taken into account. The moderation material had to include these details when demonstrating a level to give a clear picture of the pupil's overall functioning.

Could a judgement be made on one piece of evidence?

All practitioners sitting on this panel felt that one piece of work was not adequate to make an assessment of their overall progress and attainment. When teachers make assessments for those pupils functioning within the National Curriculum levels, they use their professional knowledge of the child and their work and progress over time, so why should it be any different for those pupils functioning at the P-levels? The group felt that for each pupil being moderated, a pen picture of the individual should be submitted including their rate of progress, learning styles in many learning environments and the support over time. This picture should support a number of pieces of work that demonstrate all elements of the P-level. By doing it this way, the journey the pupil has taken to reach their current level of achievement is displayed.

Should the materials within the moderation pack be different for different genders/ages/schools?

It was evident when studying the work from the pupils, that there were marked differences between gender, age and school even within the same level. It was agreed that a combination of material should be put into the moderation pack to ensure that all teachers could see the varying ways children can present even within one P-level.

The moderation pack was devised to support mainstream colleagues with children working between P4 and P8. This received positive feedback once disseminated and mainstream teachers felt they had an assessment tool to support their judgements for the minority of children who they teach.

As government and local authorities dictate, special school teachers, like their mainstream counterparts, have to make formal assessments and demonstrate that their pupils make progress over time. The difficulty is clear with those pupils functioning at the lower P-levels; that is, P1(i)–P3(ii). Many of these pupils have very complex needs, many having medical conditions that together prevent them from accessing the curriculum and/or the environment. It appears difficult for these pupils to make steady progress and in some situations any progress at all, not forgetting a small minority of pupils having regressive syndromes, which lead to the loss of skills over time. There are of course assessment tools on the market that break each P-level down in each subject strand and this allows teachers to demonstrate that pupils may make progress within a P-level but do not always move onto the next. These tools provide a means to show small-step progress. However, even with the small steps within a level, some pupils, because of their difficulties, will not meet expectations.

Where a pupil or a cohort of pupils with similar difficulties struggle to meet elements of the criteria for a given level, in collaboration with other professionals, it is often deemed necessary to allow them to move on to the next level having partially achieved the previous one.

The P-levels do demonstrate, on the other hand, that the majority of our children with Special Educational Needs do make progress. This supports special schools in demonstrating good teaching and learning practices.

Pressure is usually put on schools by government and LAs who expect both special and mainstream schools to show value-added results and justify their existence in terms of quality teaching and learning. While mainstream schools have always had standardised tests to meet this expectation, special schools had no national testing system until the P scales were published in 1998. Therefore, using the P scales, special schools can now show pupils' attainment and progress and can, through constant moderation, ensure that there is consistency in assessment across schools and at all levels of the P scales.

It is hoped that this case study has highlighted some of the advantages of using the P scales as well as the drawbacks. It is also hoped that the case study involving one LA gives a good insight into the type of assistance teachers (especially inexperienced teachers) need in their quest to maintain consistency while using the P scales.

John Parkes – Springfield Special School for Pupils with Complex Learning Needs, Cawthorne Close, Knowsley, Merseyside

Springfield Special School provides educational opportunities for pupils aged 2–19 with complex learning needs.

At Springfield Special School, the ability range demonstrated by the school population has always presented a challenge when assessing the in-depth educational progress made by the pupils. All pupils have a level of physical disability, which impacts on their rate of learning, further complicated by either moderate, severe or profound and multiple learning difficulties (PMLD).

It is within this context that staff have diligently worked for years to provide the best possible educational journey for pupils, though not exclusively, without the clarity and support needed from central government. The school is not unique in this respect as many special and inclusive mainstream schools have experienced the same levels of challenge and frustration when trying to meet the needs of pupils with Special Educational Needs.

With the introduction of the P scales framework by the QCA in 2001, a platform for measuring attainment for pupils who progress at a slower rate was created and with it, the possibility of analysing progress data for pupils with SEN. The school has been part of this journey and has used the comparative data created by CEM at Durham University from the initial pilot undertaken by them on behalf of the QCA. The system of analysis has increased in sophistication with the introduction of comparative value-added data, and, hopefully, so has the skill demonstrated by the school in using this data to inform self-evaluation.

The P scales journey at Springfield Special School has several facets to it. Each is explored in turn with a concluding reflection on how this all fits into school self-evaluation. An attempt is made to identify any factors relating to the P scales, pupil progress and data analysis that may need to be addressed within future school and, possibly, national provision.

A history of implementation of the P scales at Springfield Special School

Prior to the introduction of the P scales in 1998, special schools the length and breadth of England and Wales expended enormous amounts of time and effort in the interpretation and application of the National Curriculum (Department for Education and Science 1991). Unlike our mainstream cousins, direct application of the subject attainment targets to pupils with learning difficulties was difficult at best and impossible most of the time.

Fagg et al. (1990), in 'Entitlement for all: A broad, balanced and relevant curriculum for pupils with severe and complex needs' and their subsequent subject-based support for differentiation, led the way in breaking down the National Curriculum into achievable steps. These steps took Attainment Targets at Level 1 in Maths, English and Science and split them into smaller stages so progress could be measured for those pupils referred to as working 'below Level 1'.

At Springfield Special School during this time, subject co-ordinators analysed the attainment targets and applied the process of differentiation to them. Smaller and smaller steps were created so that pupils at the lowest developmental levels could access the National Curriculum. A massive expenditure of time and effort resulted in a curriculum that was appropriate to pupils with learning difficulties. Similar undertakings were occurring elsewhere. There was little or no intervention from Government, resulting in unique, needs-led approaches and documentation. From a positive perspective, pupils could be shown to be making progress, planning was more appropriate and was linked to pupil achievement through the National Record of Achievement held for each pupil. However, there were significant weaknesses inherent in this approach.

With the growth in aspiration to include pupils with learning difficulties in mainstream schools and the subsequent pupil mobility between schools, individualised differentiated curricula proved problematic. Added to this, there was increased dissatisfaction with a national assessment system that defined pupils as 'W' meaning working towards Level 1 of the National Curriculum. For many of these pupils this deficit label would stay with them for their educational career and presented parents with their child as being a non-achiever. There was a need for change in approach at national, local and school level.

Standardisation in assessment, reporting and recording of pupils with learning difficulties became a discussion point which gained momentum. Schools looked to the creation of a common framework and language that would track pupils through their education and across schools. In addition, the framework needed to be positive and focus on 'can do and achieve' rather than the existing deficit model of the 'W' (working towards Level 1). After consultation and trialling by Government, the P scales were published by the QCA in 1998.

At Springfield Special School, the P scales were welcomed and rapidly implemented. Our lowest level differentiation referred to as 'The Access Curriculum' was retained to allow further breakdown and demonstrate progress with PMLD pupils who fell within Levels P1 to P3. At this stage, a whole school approach was developed to support pupil progress, tracking from ages 2 to 19 and across the ability range using the P scales as a mechanism but with a need to create steps within the P scales so that all progress was recognised no matter how small.

Tracking pupil progress

Using a whole-school approach that involved curriculum co-ordinators and the Senior Management Team, P scales application in smaller steps was investigated. Three substantive commercial systems became available within 18 months to 2 years of the introduction of the P scales, PACE (P scales Assessment of the National Curriculum from EQUALS), PIVATS (Performance Indicators for Value Added Target Setting) formulated by Lancashire County Council and P-Steps/Small Steps created by B-Squared. Each was critically evaluated by staff in terms of their ability to provide suitable progressions for all of our pupil population and how effectively they could track progress from the ages of 2 to 19 and across bands of learning difficulty. Whilst all three systems have merit in their own right and are now used extensively up and down the country, the B-Squared P-Steps/Small Steps best met our needs.

P-Steps/Small Steps provided suitable gradation from P1 of the P scales to Level 4 of the National Curriculum in Maths, Science, English and PSHE. As a paper-driven system, it allowed all staff to establish a baseline level of functioning for their pupils, which significantly aided the setting of appropriate progression targets. Individual Educational Plans (IEPs) or Individual Action Plans (IAPs) at Springfield Special School, became far more focused, demonstrating real progress to parents. In doing so, the 'working towards Level 1 (W)' deficit model of recording pupil progress was challenged with a greater emphasis on how much pupils with SEN could achieve. This in turn made for a more positive Annual Review of a pupil's statement of special educational need.

Consistent application of this system across the school meant that pupil progress transferred from class to class with the movement of the child throughout their educational career at the school. The later transfer of the B-Squared material into a management information system referred to as 'Connected Steps', again produced by B-Squared, further enhanced the opportunities for tracking pupil progress against the P scales. Reports could be generated when wanted and progression percentage within a P-Level could be demonstrated. At last, staff could recognise even the tiniest progression made by a pupil and demonstrate this to each other, parents, governors and, during inspection, to Ofsted.

Issues still existed around the ability to provide consistent views of the progress made by pupils. Staff attempted to moderate their decisions using exemplars of work produced by pupils at the school, but this proved to be a very time-consuming process. With the introduction of the 'Making That Step' and 'Making That Step 2' P scales exemplification materials by Devon Curriculum Services, high-quality moderating materials were made available. This CD-based resource could be used with individuals, groups or whole staff to support and validate any P scales Levels attributed to pupils at the school. In addition, it had been developed in association with B-Squared and, as such, dovetailed into the Connecting Steps system for recording pupil progress. The school had obtained a pupil progress tracking system with which it felt secure and which was evaluated very highly by the staff. Connecting Steps was generating large amounts of data about all the pupils in the school, data which could easily be applied and analysed.

P scales data analysis

The National Curriculum Attainment Levels obtained by pupils at End of Key Stages 1, 2 and 3 and their statutory reporting to national government provided a wealth of statistical data through which mainstream primary and secondary schools could compare their performance with others. Through the PANDA, e-PANDA and recently Raise-online as well as Fischer Family Trust data, they were, and are, able to review how well their pupils attain. Local Authorities and OFSTED have been able to challenge and grade school performance, all of which has been achievable due to the relative homogeneity in the mainstream pupil population.

The enormous variation in performance and non-homogenous nature of the SEN pupil population made the statistical analysis of SEN pupil data problematic. However, the introduction of the P scales as a common framework for analysis as well as a clearer banding and definition of categories of SEN, made this process more viable for schools like Springfield Special School.

A body of special schools and mainstream schools with special units were invited by the QCA to take part in a piece of research undertaken on their behalf by the CEM at Durham University. Springfield Special School was one of the invited schools. The pilot study banded pupil P scales levels by year group and ability band, for example Severe Learning Difficulty pupils at year groups R to Y11. After collation of the data, schools were provided with graphical representation of their comparative data so they could compare and contrast their pupils with other similar pupils from across the country. A lower and upper inter-quartile range was defined allowing analysis of relatively high performing pupils and those lower performing for whom additional educational intervention may be needed. At Springfield Special School, the B-squared P-Steps and Small Steps pupil progress levels transferred easily into the QCA/CEM data requirements and provided quality comparative data.

After the QCA pilot ceased, CEM continued to provide the comparative data analysis to schools who wished to participate, expanding what was available to include value-added comparative data based on relative pupil progress across a two-year period. Springfield Special School maintained and expanded its data analysis through the links to CEM, refining the use of data to inform aspects of its self-evaluation of performance.

Application of the P scales in school self-evaluation

As Ofsted inspections became more sophisticated with requirements made of schools to demonstrate their performance, the process of self-evaluation gained momentum. Schools were expected to complete the school Self-Evaluation Form (SEF), a document that became the bedrock of data collection by Ofsted prior to inspecting a school. It was the content of the SEF and the grade allocated by the school to its performance that could be challenged by Ofsted in the form of a Pre-Inspection Brief.

In summer 2005, the DFES invited schools to report pupil progress in terms of P scales, a requirement that became legislative under the DCSF in September 2007. Since then, all schools have had to define the attainment of pupils previously working towards Level 1 of the National Curriculum by the application of the P scales. It is this assessment and reporting of P scales that is now intrinsic in self-evaluation in special schools.

At Springfield Special School, school self-evaluation is a detailed cyclical process, involving the use of pupils' P scales data to show progress at individual, end of Key Stage, cohort and whole school levels. Whole school target setting has probed deeper and deeper into subsections of Maths, English and Science so that the targets provide a challenge to staff and pupils whilst being meaningful not tokenistic. The CEM P scales Project data, both comparative and value-added allow outward looking analysis, comparing and contrasting with others and asking questions about performance. The combination of whole school targets, the comparative data, value-added data and individual targets set in Individual Education Plans (IAPs at Springfield Special School) provide an analytical and interconnected source of self-evaluation that is of vital importance when applied within the school Self-Evaluation Form. Such data is used by governors, the headteacher and subject co-ordinators in Maths, Science, English and PSHE to challenge the curriculum and its application at individual, departmental and whole school levels. During an OFSTED inspection in 2005, it was fundamental in gaining the school an outstanding OFSTED verdict in all areas.

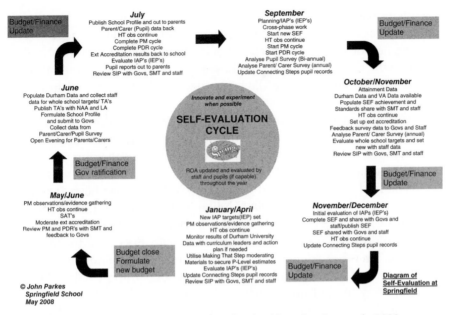

Figure 5.4: Springfield Special School self-evaluation cycle 2008.

Figure 5.4 shows the Springfield Special School Self-Evaluation Cycle and identifies all aspects applied by the school to self-evaluation during the academic year.

During the formation of the Self-Evaluation Cycle at Springfield Special School and in subsequent work with a sister federated school, it has become clear that there are still significant areas in need of development within Early Years and Post 16 provision. The P scales and their application still face challenges in the future.

Limitations of the P scales and future challenges

Despite the high quality of the CEM P scales project and other similar projects such as PIVATS and EQUALS, for the pupils with the most complex Special Educational Needs the process of comparative data analysis is still an inexact science. Such pupils cannot be easily banded into ability ranges, often bridging across several with additional factors impacting, such as mental health problems. In the analysis of any comparative data for these pupils, care should be taken in being too literal in drawing conclusions. As is demonstrated in the Springfield Special School Self-Evaluation Cycle Diagram, cross-referencing several sources of data can provide a greater depth to analysis. Schools should look for trends and probe for causative factors as they relate to their unique situation and use the comparative data obtained by them as a tool in this process.

Changes in The Foundation Stage, which relate to children aged 0–5, and exploration of Diplomas for Post 16 aged students both provide new challenges when applied to children and young people with Special Educational Needs.

The Early Years Foundation Stage (EYFS) 0–5 has been further defined by the DCSF in 2008. Unlike its predecessor, the learning goals in the EYFS 0–5 now extend to very early child development. This allows its application to children with Special Educational Needs. It has been developed alongside the Primary Framework for Literacy and Mathematics so that the Early Learning Goals (ELGs) link to Key Stage 1 and transition between EYFS and the National Curriculum is facilitated. No consideration has been given by the DCSF to transition for those pupils who will undertake their educational career within the P scales. As such, a suggested future development should be the mapping of the EYFS with the P scales so that transition at early years is inclusive of all pupils.

Provision for students with SEN beyond the age of 16 allows freedom of curriculum delivery outside of the National Curriculum. External accreditation for work undertaken by such students is extensive, utilises their progression on the P scales and allows them to demonstrate their ability to achieve. However, national data collection has failed to recognise externally accredited schemes unless they relate to GCSE, NVQ or GNVQ and funding from the Learning Skills Council has not been accessible.

Fortunately, the development of the Qualification and Credit Framework (QCF) by the QCA in 2008 may have allowed for the inclusion of students with SEN in nationally recognised qualifications for the first time. Within the QCF, the diploma structure has identified a Foundation Learning Tier Diploma (FLTD) that is differentiated at a level that includes students with Special Educational Needs. The functional skills aspect of the FLTD that addresses English, ICT and Maths is pitched so that P scales attainment levels can be included within its requirements. In September 2008,

Springfield Special School was included in the national pilot of this diploma. The evolution of the FLTD has the capability to include Post 16 SEN students at a national level hitherto unavailable. It is the aspiration of Springfield Special School and other similar schools involved in the development of the diploma to catalyse P scales progression made by pupils into meaningful, recognised qualifications for post-school life.

Ginny Brown – Montacute School, Canford Heath Road, Poole

Who we are

Montacute School is an all age (3–19) SLD PMLD school situated in the unitary authority of Poole. All of our pupils have Severe or Profound and Multiple Learning Difficulties and many have additional difficulties such as sensory impairment, physical disability or Autistic Spectrum Disorder (ASD).

Our history with P scales

In common with many special schools, we began assessing pupils using P scales right from the start, pleased that at last our pupils were on the spectrum of achievement. Before the introduction of P scales in 1998, we were frustrated that our pupils were assessed as 'W' (working towards Level 1) for all of their school lives even though we knew they were making stupendous achievements. We welcomed the opportunity for this achievement to be recognised, celebrated and to provide a baseline. We have been through the usual difficulties of understanding what the P scales are all about, how to make sense of the data they have generated and moderation; some teachers being very generous and others very strict.

What we do now

Teachers, together with the speech and language therapist and sometimes the assessment, recording and reporting coordinator and subject coordinators, assess pupils annually against P scales.

We do not publish this information to parents on an annual basis unless they particularly ask. We keep long-term records of pupil progress, with P scales broken down so that the small steps within P scales can be seen. We have not used PIVATS or B-Squared, being worried about the temptation to 'teach to' these systems. Curriculum co-ordinators draw up long- and medium-term schemes of work based on subject content and using P scales as an assessment tool, although we use the subjects as vehicles for Key Skills assessment too.

We compare each year's assessment with the year before and see how many children, or groups of children, made progress within their levels, moved to the next level or moved down a level. This can lead to questions being asked about why children or groups of children have performed as they have done.

Other assessments

We use many other assessments including those recommended by the speech and language therapists and the occupational therapist.

We have a Key Skills recording and assessment programme, which we developed over many years with the whole staff team, and we use this to prepare IEP (Individual Education Plan) targets. These are cross-curricular skills and we drew on the QCA (2001) booklet, *Developing Skills,* and materials from Woodland School in Essex as a starting point. This recording system is very different from tick box systems and includes teachers giving real, dated examples of when a child achieves a certain skill. We find this very useful for report writing and parents say they prefer this to being given a P scales assessment for their child.

How we use P scales and the difficulties we have had

We have been keeping records of P scales assessments for several years, and it is possible to look at individual and group trends now. Two things have prevented this information from being useful: firstly, P scales being recalibrated in 2004; and, secondly, the fact that in the past we rounded pupils to the nearest P scale, whether higher or lower. Now we always round down.

For example, we would assign a numerical value to each P scale:

P1(i)	1
P1(ii)	2
P2(i)	3
P2(ii)	4
P3(i)	5
P3(ii)	6
P4	7
P5	8
P6	9
P7	10
P8	11

so a pupil could score:

'Writing'	P4 = 7
'Speaking and listening'	P5 = 8
'Reading'	P5 = 8
Total:	23/3 = 7.6

The nearest P scale is P5 so the pupil would be assessed as overall P5.

Now, we round all numbers down to the nearest P scale, so the same pupil would be assessed in English overall as being at P4. This and the recalibration have made comparisons over the years meaningless. In effect we started again in 2005.

What we do with our data

We send our assessment data to CEM at Durham University who prepare it for us. We are able to see graphs of the progress of individual pupils and cohorts compared with national data. This is interesting and is the first time we have been able to access comparative data. It gives us a broad picture of how our pupils are doing against similar pupils across the country. The number of pupils in each national cohort varies enormously and it needs to be remembered that we are not looking at how our pupils have done against all pupils nationally but against pupils whose data have been submitted, anything from tens of pupils to a few hundred. It is also difficult to know who our children are being compared with; are our ASD pupils being compared with more able ASD pupils? Our PMLD pupils always do well against the Durham data but maybe our definition of PMLD is different from that in other parts of the country. The value added data provided by Durham is also interesting, and we particularly appreciate the recent highlighting that indicates whether a pupil has performed above, below or as expected. This information has not, so far, shown up any surprises or worries. I think that, in a small special school, the pupils are so well known to the staff that we already understand the levels they are working at and are very aware when they are having a difficult time or not making the progress they should. The new software from CEM has also proved interesting, giving us the option of comparing the progress of girls with that of boys for example. We agree with the latest Ofsted guidance that starting points and past performance are the best predictors of achievement and are less confident that cohorts of categories of need are useful.

Moderation

Moderation is crucial in assessment and target setting. We have worked hard on this over the years and are beginning to find it easier to reach consensus as a team of teachers, teaching assistants and speech and language therapists. We meet for a series of sessions in the spring term to bring pieces of work (description, annotated photo or video clip) to be assessed by the group. This piece of work is filed and dated along with the assessment proforma (adapted from the materials provided by EMSEN (East Midlands Special Education group) and is stored as a bank of moderated work for teachers to refer to. In practice, I don't think this evidence is referred to as a way of supporting assessment, and I don't think teachers focus too much on whether someone is a P5 or a P6, but the process of talking about individual children as a group and observing and assessing together is very valuable. It has been very useful to work with other schools in moderation too. Our English and Mathematics co-ordinators attend moderation meetings for their subjects, the Borough of Poole arranges cross-Borough moderation meetings and Dorset County Council's inspector for inclusion arranges moderation meetings for special schools across Dorset, Bournemouth and Poole.

Target setting

P scales were developed to facilitate target setting for pupils with SEN. We feel we have made an honest attempt to do this but problems such as pupils' spiky profiles and the effects that medication, illness and hospital stays can have on pupils make it difficult to predict five terms ahead. We revisit the targets half way through the cycle to see if we are on track and this can have implications for teaching. For example, if we set a target for a child to achieve level P7 in 'Shape, space and measure', the teacher may focus on using the language 'forwards and backwards' in different contexts, to help the child achieve the target. We set targets in teams of people who teach the child, including speech and language therapists and teaching assistants. We have found we are getting more accurate at predicting where we can get a child to achieve but our teachers are instructed to be honest, ambitious, to look at trends, to consider the child's circumstance (target setting is always done for individuals and then translated into cohorts), to talk to each other and make their best professional judgements. There is always a tension between setting targets that are challenging enough that children may not achieve and easier targets that are achievable but may not be developmental for the child.

Materials

Materials we have found useful include the EMSEN materials, which are particularly useful for training and for moderation, especially the examples of moderated work. We have also used 'The use of performance criteria in the assessment of speaking and listening' by Derby City, and The General Guidelines, Using the P scales and Developing Skills booklets from the QCA.

We really liked the National Literacy Strategy and National Numeracy Strategy booklets 'Towards the National Curriculum', which aren't any use since the P scales were recalibrated, and also 'Supporting the Target setting process' – both editions – because we like the 15 point steps for PSD in the original version.

What we find useful about P scales

We know that pieces of work are assessed, not the child, but it can be useful to describe a child as, for example, 'around the P8'level'. It gives us a rough idea of the level the pupil is working at.

Sometimes a trend can be seen – maybe a dip in progress at a key stage or in a subject. When we have investigated this in depth, looking at individual pupil progress, the explanation is always clear- there has been a stay in hospital, changes at home, a 'surge' in the previous year or behaviour problems getting in the way of progress. The value in interrogating the data so deeply has been the opportunity to talk as a staff team about individual pupils and how they can best be supported. An outcome has sometimes been a change of emphasis in the pupil's curriculum – the addition of music therapy, for example, or an emphasis on broadening experience rather than linear progress.

We do assess pupils using P scales from the age of 4 to post 16 although we are aware of the guidance regarding the Foundation Stage. We find it gives us a starting and end point for our pupils and a common language across this 3–19 school. Some interesting discussions we have had have been around how P7, for example, can look very different in upper school or lower school or indeed in a mainstream school.

Inclusion and outreach

Because the school provides an outreach service and because we have inclusion link schools across the Borough, many of our teachers and our speech and language therapist spend time in mainstream schools. As well as the many benefits to both sets of children, this helps us to keep us in touch with what typically developing children are like, what levels they are working at and how they are being assessed. Having P scales has given us a common language with our mainstream colleagues and has helped us to see our children on a continuum rather than being 'other'. However, our outreach teachers tend to use our Key Skills system rather than P scales to help mainstream teachers support their pupils' development.

The frustrations of using P scales

How do we assess pupils in PSHE (which we consider to be the most important area of the curriculum) above P8? We liked the 'old' 15-point scale and would like to go back to using it.

The Judging Achievement expectations that Ofsted inspectors reportedly look at is problematic when P scales are widely different from each other; for example, when they look to the number of levels gained in a key stage.

In 'Number', P4 contains 1 element:

1. Pupils show an awareness of number activities and counting.

P6 contains seven elements:

1. Pupils demonstrate an understanding of 1–1 correspondence in a range of contexts
2. Pupils join in rote counting to 5
3. They count reliably to 3
4. They make sets of up to 3 objects
5. They use numbers in familiar games and activities
6. They demonstrate an understanding of the concept of 'more'
7. They join in with new number rhymes, songs, stories and games.

If a pupil makes progress from P3(ii) to P4 is that the same as from P5 to P6?

The levels don't always seem to correspond with typical development. Many pupils are unable to complete a level because of their particular difficulties and 'spiky profiles'.

There are still some anomalies such as 'matching objects' occurring at P5 in Science and at P4 in 'Shape, space and measures'.

It is still difficult to compare the performance of one special school with another, although, as stated in *Setting targets for pupils with Special Educational Needs* (Ofsted 2004) 'there is value in comparing the progress of pupils of similar ability at the same age and starting point in different schools'.

Cohorts can be extremely small and statistically meaningless. One year our cohort of Year 10 pupils comprised 1 pupil.

We don't teach in subjects, particularly in lower school, so we find our own Key Skills method of recording progress more useful than National Curriculum subject assessments – even using P scales.

We are aware that P scales are indicators and that assessment should be 'best fit'; however, we still get stuck when trying to assess pupils or to set the statutory targets five terms ahead. We have particular problems assessing pupils whose difficulties mean they may never achieve all elements in a P scale; for instance, pupils with autism could be taught to 'seek help when needed' (PSHE P8) but may never master 'begin to respond to the feelings of others' (PSHE P4) or 'make purposeful relationships with others in group activities' (PSHE P7). We have had many debates amongst ourselves: do we go with 'best fit' and move them on or leave them stuck at P4 for their school lives? We tend to go for 'the best fit' option now, sometimes putting a note on the pupil's records to explain which element they may not have achieved and why. This dilemma is recognised by the DCSF and on the Standards Site 'How children make progress', which says: 'teachers will need to make professional judgements as to whether these "gaps" or barriers can be overcome ... or acknowledge that a specific aspect of learning may continue to be a learning target, whilst other aspects of learning continue to progress'.

How we don't use P scales

Our pupils are in age-grouped classes of widely mixed abilities. P scales can be useful in that teachers have an immediate understanding of the range if they can see that their class is performing at between P3(ii) and P8 for example, and they give a broad idea of the planning needed. But while pupils are sometimes split into needs-led groups, P scales are never used to group pupils.

Final comments

We see the P scales assessments as just part of the picture of assessing pupils, along with our own observations, feedback from parents and carers and other assessments. We try not to give P scales assessments more importance than they are due in a school where the pupils' emotional and physical wellbeing can be more of a priority than progress in P scales. However, we have seen the introduction and development of P scales as a very welcome move in including children who have Special Educational Needs.

Di Brown – Springfield School, Crewe Green Road, Crewe

Introduction

Professionals working in the field of learning difficulties have always been users and producers of assessment tools. Well before the advent of a formal National Curriculum a plethora of assessment tools existed covering a vast range of skills, areas and specific difficulties. For many years individual schools have selected their own personal favourites, the ones that measured their own personal specialisms or those that were in vogue at the time. Individual schools made good use of these tools but communication, collaboration and comparison between schools was very difficult.

Until the introduction of the QCA's P scales assessment criteria none of the assessments had allowed or assisted special schools to assess their pupils appropriately on their progress in areas of the National Curriculum. Pupils in special education were generally scored at 'W' or 'working towards Level 1', which allowed no distinction between the lowest and highest attainers and no measure of progress within 'working towards Level 1'. The introduction of the P scales was the first opportunity for schools to use a national, standardised tool to assess pupils working towards and within Level 1 of the National Curriculum and, more importantly, to measure and demonstrate their progress.

Springfield is an all aged special school for pupils and young people with severe to profound and multiple learning difficulties. Like most schools of its type, in reality the pupils have a wide range of increasingly more complex needs.

Assessments process

Springfield school pupils have been assessed annually using the P scales assessment criteria since 1998 and the wealth of data generated from this has been interrogated and subjected to scrutiny, which at times seems to raise more questions than it answers.

Each pupil up to Year 12 is assessed using the P scales in May of each year – to coincide with SATs. We made the decision to include pupils in the Foundation Stage as, for our pupils, the National

Foundation Stage Profile provides insufficient useful information and because we wanted to be able to accurately measure progress between the Foundation Stage and Key Stage 1 – which we feel necessitates the use of the same assessment profile in each stage.

Staff are asked to make best-fit judgements using a criteria of success based on pupils achieving 70% of the level descriptors, 70% of the time. They are also expected to make these judgements in class teams so as to provide first line moderation. Teaching staff then get together to moderate at school level although this can be difficult, as differing levels of experience and knowledge of pupils can still cause opinions to be swayed. The experience of most staff in the use of the P scales has now shown to make judgements more consistent, although we do still have some concerns over inconsistencies in judgements with some staff – particularly those with less experience, but also those with specific subject expertise. On the whole, when colleagues become familiar and experienced in applying the scales they find them easy to use.

Recently we have introduced a termly assessment tracker document. Staff are required to briefly revisit each pupil's previous assessment and judge approximate progress. The aim of this exercise is to target additional or alternative input for pupils apparently making slow or insufficient progress, and to identify pupils who have already reached the target levels set for them, so as to set additional targets. This aims to keep the assessment levels more in the forefront of teachers' minds and to keep their individual pupil objectives more focused towards encouraging measurable progress through the levels.

P level assessments are also reported annually through the Annual Pupil Progress Report and to the Local Authority and parents through the Annual Review of Statement. Parents generally appreciate the data they are given and, as we include a brief guide to the levels, understand what the scores indicate. On a regular basis we use graphical representations of progress in order to give a visual picture, which is often more useful and powerful.

The graphical feedback from the P scales project run by CEM at Durham University is very useful to the school, showing clearly where our school is achieving in the 'bigger picture'. Initially the graphs were mainly used by the leadership team to analyse data and target additional support, but these graphs are increasingly being used by other staff. They, and the other analysis provided by the CEM team, also proved particularly useful when we had our recent Ofsted Inspection.

Problems in using the P scales

Over the years the use of the scales has not been without its difficulties – some of which relate to the scales themselves rather than the individuals or settings using them. With revisions to the scales some of the difficulties have been resolved, some remain and some have been created.

Initial difficulties with the early levels P1 to P3 were improved with revision, breaking down the levels into sub sections, but for many pupils with profound and multiple learning difficulties it is still often difficult for the pupil to progress from one level to the next. This has caused many schools to turn to schemes such as PIVATS or B-Squared – either as alternative assessments or as supportive assessments – and this in turn can create difficulties in moderation between schools. Movement between levels at other specific points also proves difficult – specifically from P3(ii) to P4 and from P8 to NC1 – and again schools often ease this problem through the use of alternative schemes.

Another problem is the occasional disparity between levels in terms of the subtlety or interpretation of the language or, on occasions, the number or rigour of the assessment statements. For example, P4 in 'Number' has just a single, fairly broad assessment statement 'Pupils show an interest in number activities and counting', whilst in the same strand P6 has five statements and the generic maths level P3(i) contains eight statements – all of which are far more specific.

Rigour and parity are also concerns in the area of science. Here this relates, not directly to the assessment scales themselves, but to their relationship with the National Curriculum levels. Our school is fortunate to have a science teacher who has taught the subject in both mainstream and special schools and has raised concerns over the rigour of the assessment scales after P8. The concern is that the wording of the levels may lead non-specialist subject teachers to credit pupils with levels that are considerably higher than would be awarded by a trained science specialist thus artificially 'raising' the attainment of some pupils. This leads to problems in standardisation – especially where pupils move schools or are dual rolled with a mainstream school. Within our own school we have had issues where non-specialist subject primary department teachers make assessments in science which the secondary specialist science teacher is unable to agree with – resulting in apparent regression of skills for some pupils when they move into Key Stage 3.

Changes and refinements to the levels over the years have also been a mixed blessing. Whilst some of the changes were very beneficial to both assessors and assessed, others have had quite negative impacts. Major changes to the wording of level descriptors has again led to some pupils apparently 'regressing' – even by several levels over the course of some years (as in PSHE) and this can be difficult to explain to stakeholders and Ofsted colleagues.

The change which initially separated speaking and listening was very warmly welcomed and was felt to give us a far more useful assessment. However the subsequent re-combining of the speaking and listening strands after P8 has caused us major problems as many of our pupils have vastly differing scores in the two areas, particularly where the pupil has a hearing impairment or a communication difficulty. We therefore continue to use the separate scales but have to aggregate the two scores to send data to the CEM P scales project and the DCSF. This affects the accuracy of the data.

Reporting problems also occur where pupils have significantly different scores between strands – for example, pupils with 'speaking' and 'listening' scores at P4 and above but 'reading' and 'writing' scores in the generic levels (P1–P3), or those with some scores in the P levels and some in NC levels. There seems to be an expectation, at least in some reporting formats, that pupils will achieve similar scores in each strand of a particular subject and this is not the case, certainly with a large number of our pupils who have 'spikey' profiles of development.

By far our biggest concern has been the changes to the PSHE assessments. The initial three strands – 'Personal skills', 'Working with others' and 'Independent skills' – were changed to 'Interacting and working with others', 'Independent and organisational skills' and 'Attention', each having different descriptors. This caused a number of our pupils to have quite significant changes to their assessments. An even less helpful change came when these three levels were reduced to just a single strand for PSHE. For many pupils in our school, the area in which they can often make the biggest and most significant progress is PSHE. Having a single assessment strand does not allow them to demonstrate this progress fully and does not reflect the true complex nature of the personal skills of some groups of pupils. For example, the previous three-strand assessment clearly showed the variations in abilities between the strands of pupils with Autistic Spectrum Disorders – generally showing much lower levels in working with others – but the three strands enabled them to demonstrate progress in other areas, even if their ability to work with others remained the same or deterio-rated. A single strand cannot fully reflect the work of a school such as ours in this area and so some schools – ourselves included – continue to use the three-strand scale, sending an aggregated (and therefore less accurate) level for data collection.

Benefits of using the P scales

In general, P scales have proved to be a valuable tool and the analy-sis that we receive from the CEM at Durham University further adds to their usefulness.

In summary the benefits are:

- The levels provide a unifying means of compiling quantitative data on pupil progress in the core subjects, allowing the school to track and analyse individual, class, key stage and whole school trends.
- The feedback we receive from the project then allows us to bench-mark and compare our data with other schools and to monitor aspects of the education which we as a school provide.
- Using the P scales data we can monitor the effects on our pupils' progress of a range of school and national initiatives, report in a meaningful way to parents, the local authority, other agencies and the DCSF, and share attainment information between schools in a common 'language'.
- The data can be used to set meaningful targets – for individual pupils, for the school and in the context of performance manage-ment of staff.

- We also find the value added analysis provided by the CEM very useful, and again the use of colours to show higher and lower performing pupils provides a powerful visual tool. This information allows us to look at strengths, areas for development and trends in the performance of pupils.
- We are currently working with the predictions information, which is proving less useful when applied annually as it is more geared to achievement over key stages. Annual predictions often cannot be used as this would need assessment of half or thirds of levels – although schools who also use assessment tools such as PIVATS or B-Squared could possibly supplement this information to gain annual predictions.

Conclusion

In conclusion, the introduction of the P scales has been very successful for our school. We are delighted to be able to demonstrate and celebrate the progress made by pupils – and conversely investigate, challenge or explain apparent lack of progress or regression. We are able to report this progress to parents and the authorities using a common language which aids conversation. The use of the P scales and the Durham Project's analysis has helped to bring the schools' assessment, recording and reporting procedures into sharper focus. As a result, this has enabled us to ensure that we set achievable but challenging targets for pupils and the school, and has supported us in our dialogues with our School Improvement Partner. The data and its analysis also supported our school self-assessment process and helped us to be judged an 'outstanding' school by Ofsted (2005 and 2008).

Bernie Tetchner – Lark Hall Centre for Pupils with Autism, Smedley Street, London

Using P levels has helped us to focus on assessment of pupils and to plan the next steps in what a pupil should be achieving.

We have arranged our curriculum into topics such as 'Myself' and 'Changes'. We use Equals Schemes of Work/Strategies, where the content is organised progressively through the P levels, to inform our long-term planning. We use PIVATS where each of the P levels has been broken down into five parts to inform the steps that we take in helping the pupils achieve part of a P level or a whole P level.

Knowledge of the pupils' P scales attainment levels informs our weekly planning and since our classes are quite small – seven pupils – we can plan very tightly. Teachers' knowledge of P levels means that we can extend pupils into the next level.

We use a range of formative and summative assessments to measure the pupils' achievements. The formative assessments include observations (incidental and focused), photographs, videos, etc., which are matched against the P levels and the five parts of each P level in PIVATS. At the end of the academic year we use Equals PACE2 to assess our pupils summatively. Similar to mainstream KS1 and KS2 SATs, we are aware that these PACE2 assessments can be 'snapshots' of the pupils' achievements. PACE2 results as well as observations and evidence build up over the year to inform our decisions to award a particular P level.

We have been submitting our results to CEM at Durham University for a number of years. The feedback that we get is very useful. Firstly, we can track individual pupils over time. This informs our knowledge and planning for an individual pupil. Some pupils show year-on-year progression in all areas. Other pupils do not show progression in all areas. We can then analyse this data and plan more closely to help the pupil make progress.

Since we are an ASD provision the areas that our pupils find challenging are the language/communication/abstract areas. They generally do well in number and reading (whilst it is still at the word recognition levels as in P5, P6 and P7). As the curriculum subjects require more abstract thought, interpretation, deduction and emotional engagement they find these areas challenging. The value added data provided for each pupil is useful and we can see where a pupil is making good progress and where others are not.

CEM compares our results with other ASD provision across the country and it is helpful for us to see our results compared with theirs. It would be good to know the range of learning difficulty that other pupils have who are also diagnosed with ASD.

PIVATS has broken down the P levels for writing into five strands; that is, text focus, language/grammar focus, spelling focus, vocabulary focus and motor focus. This is very useful for us as some of our pupils can achieve some of these strands for a particular focus but not others and so we can show progress in these strands. It would be useful to have more of the National Curriculum levels broken down into smaller steps and for this to be agreed nationally.

Jo Gilbert and Mary Adossides – Manor School, Chamberlayne Road, Kensal Rise, London

Manor School has been using P scales as an assessment tool since 1999. Teachers assess their pupils as part of their annual review report and the Individual Education Plan (IEP) is set using P scales at the annual review conference.

P scales are collected at the beginning of each academic year to tackle possible issues of moderation and in preparation for performance management meetings. They are also collected in April in preparation for sending them to Equals/Durham for analysis. These results are analysed by staff to inform the annual review of standards reporting to the LA and governors. Possible discrepancies are looked for amongst different groups such as, SEN, ethnicity, gender, etc. Results are fed back and perceived under-achievement tackled through performance management.

All subjects are tracked by the administrator, reported to subject leaders and outcomes discussed with teachers at their performance management meeting. The pupils' achievement target is for teachers to achieve an average value added score or above and this is reviewed. Also teachers have been encouraged to use P scales to set targets for their children for English and Mathematics. Pupils' P level scores are used to inform class groupings annually.

Teachers are expected to use observations and PACE 2 to support their assessments. Originally teachers were encouraged to ensure a child achieves every aspect of a level before being moved up. Teachers are reviewing this and moving on to a best-fit model.

Since the school has been using P scales, consistency of assessment has been an issue and different approaches have been attempted. Recently, moderation exercises have been organised around 'Speaking and Listening', 'Writing', and 'Using and applying'. These have included looking at samples of work, video clips, gathering evidence on a child and reaching a shared agreement on what constitutes a particular P level.

P scales provide a useful developmental measure in all subject areas. They identify progress that can be reported to parents at their child's annual review conference. Some children move up a scale every year, others over two years, others make little or no progress throughout their school life. This is particularly true of pupils with very severe learning difficulties and a diagnosis of autism, whose communication skills seem to remain static. It is also true of pupils assessed on the generic P scales P (2) or P (3). Also pupils might achieve aspects of higher levels but not enough to award them the full level.

In our opinion P scales provide a more accurate baseline than the Early Years' Stepping Stones and are a better measure of progress for all pupils. Value added analysis has allowed us to ask relevant questions about our pupils' progress.

Overall our experiences have been very positive. The only issue is one of moderation.

Some of the P scales are precise and neat and even suggest strategies which can be recognised for assessment, for example 'Speaking' P4 'Repeats, copies and imitates between 10 and 50 single words, signs or phrases' or 'uses a repertoire of objects of reference or symbols'. Other level descriptors are wordy and lengthy.

At the generic levels, there needs to be more detailed assessment measures to guide teachers working with these children.

References

DES (1991) National Curriculum Subjects. London: HMSO.

Fagg S, Aherne P, Skelton S and Thornber A (1990) *Entitlement for All: A broad, balanced and relevant curriculum for pupils with severe and complex.* London: Fulton.

Ofsted (2004) *Setting Targets for Pupils with Special Educational Needs.* London: Ofsted. http://www.ofsted.gov.uk/Ofsted-home/Forms-and-guidance/Browse-all-by/Other/General/Setting-targets-for-pupils-with-special-educational-needs-Glossy-pdf

QCA (2001) *Developing Skills – Planning, teaching and assessing the curriculum for pupils with learning difficulties.* London: Qualifications and Curriculum Authority.

QCA (2007) *General Guidelines: Planning, teaching and assessing the curriculum for pupils with learning difficulties QCA & DfEE.* London: QCA Publications.

DCSF 'How children make progress', www.standards.dfes.gov.uk/ secondary/keystage3/issues/focus/pscales/history/pupilprogress

CHAPTER 6

Research into the P scales

Francis Ndaji and Peter Tymms

Since 1999 the CEM at Durham University has, in collaboration with schools conducted an annual collection and analysis of P scales assessment data. Although the primary aim of the data collection and analysis was to prepare feedback that schools would use in self-evaluation and setting pupil improvement targets, the data collected each year was also analysed and certain recurrent trends identified in the course of the analyses. The use of the feedback produced annually for schools and the general trends identified from the P scales data analysis are the subjects of this chapter.

P scales Feedback for Schools

Performance data based on the P scales criteria were obtained from pupils in special schools and mainstream schools who were known to have one or more categories of Special Educational Needs. For the purpose of analysis their P scales scores were re-coded into numbers from 1 to 16, 1 being the equivalent of P1(i) and 16 being equal to L4 of the National Curriculum.

Two sets of feedback were sent to schools each year, namely, the initial feedback and the value added feedback. The initial feedback consisted of charts and tables that compared pupils' attainment

The P scales: Assessing the Progress of Children with Special Educational Needs
Written and edited by Francis Ndaji and Peter Tymms
Copyright © 2009 John Wiley & Sons Ltd.

levels with those of similar pupils in the whole sample and in their own school. As explained in an earlier chapter, the term 'similar pupils' refers to pupils of the same year group and the same special need. The initial feedback also included a table listing pupils and their scores re-coded into numbers. Other items such as tables of predicted scores, chances graphs, percentile and data summary were added from 2005. The second set of feedback sent to schools from the P scales project was the value added feedback. The value added is, for schools, a measure of the progress each pupil makes over a period of one year. Starting from the 2007 data collection cycle, software was issued to participating schools and a new version of the software will be issued every year. The software and all the information that schools can obtain using it are described later in this chapter.

Initial feedback

The initial feedback consists of:

1. Graphs for each attainment strand in English, Mathematics and Science and one graph for PSHE for which the schools have returned pupils' P scales attainment levels.
2. Graphs for each school showing pupils' attainment levels plotted against the middle 50% of the attainment levels of all pupils reported as having the same principal need in the whole sample. For example, in each subject area there are separate graphs for PMLD, SLD and MLD, etc. The principal need involved is indicated in the chart title.
3. Graphs enabling individual pupils' attainments to be compared with those of other pupils in the school, with the school's year group average and with the performance of pupils nationally.

On the graph shown in Figure 6.1, the year groups of the pupils are shown on the x-axis (the horizontal axis). The pupil year group is identified using the National Curriculum notation and is extended to cover the 3–19 age range. For example, the assessments shown for year group 6 are those of 11-year-old pupils and those of year group 14 are those of 19-year-old pupils.

The P scales attainment levels of the pupils are on the y-axis (the vertical axis). It is a numeric scale representing the P scales range of P1(i) to National Curriculum level 4.

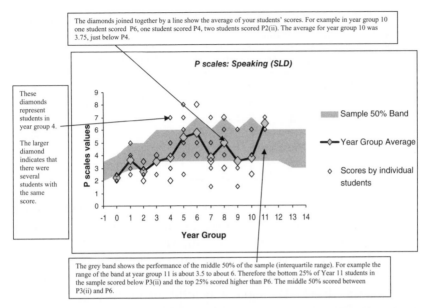

The diamonds joined together by a line show the average of your students' scores. For example in year group 10 one student scored P6, one student scored P4, two students scored P2(ii). The average for year group 10 was 3.75, just below P4.

These diamonds represent students in year group 4.

The larger diamond indicates that there were several students with the same score.

P scales: Speaking (SLD)

Sample 50% Band

Year Group Average

Scores by individual students

The grey band shows the performance of the middle 50% of the sample (interquartile range). For example the range of the band at year group 11 is about 3.5 to about 6. Therefore the bottom 25% of Year 11 students in the sample scored below P3(ii) and the top 25% scored higher than P6. The middle 50% scored between P3(ii) and P6.

Figure 6.1: Chart from the initial feedback produced for schools in the P scales data collection and analysis project. This chart is plotted from 'Speaking' scores of pupils identified as having SLD.

The unshaded diamonds represent the performances of individual pupils. The larger of these diamonds indicate that more than one pupil in that year group has scored that P level. The averages of the assessments for each year group are represented as large diamonds joined by a solid line. These also show the profile of average assessments across the year groups at the school in the subject.

The grey band represents the interquartile range or the middle 50% of the scores of each year group for the sample. A pupil whose diamond or attainment level is found above the grey band has a performance that is in the top 25% of the scores of their year group in the whole sample. Similarly, a pupil whose diamond or attainment level is found below the grey band has an attainment level that is within the bottom 25% of their year group in the whole sample. A pupil's performance in the subject under consideration is within the middle half of their year group if their attainment level is found within the grey band. Because the grey band was produced using data from the whole sample the feedback graph compares each pupil with all similar pupils. The year group

Table 6.1: List of pupils (pseudonyms used) with their P scales attainment levels re-coded into numbers

First name	Last name	Year group	Speaking	Listening	Reading	Writing
Alex	Biggs	3	2.5	2.5	4	3
Julian	Amayo	3	4	5	2	3
Lynne	Kennington	3	4	3	3.5	4
Dean	Marketer	4	2.5	3	4	3.5
James	Hammer	4	2.5	4	3.5	4
Sally	Timo	4	3	5	4	3.5

averages represented by the shaded blue diamonds can also be used in assessing whether the average group performance is above, below or within the middle 50% of the year group.

As mentioned in a previous paragraph, a table listing pupils and their P scales attainment levels re-coded into numbers is a part of the initial feedback. The table is helpful for identifying pupils on the graph. Table 6.1 can be used to identify pupils on the graph in Figure 6.1.

Suppose we want to find out how well Alex Biggs has done in 'Speaking' compared to similar pupils in the sample or in their year group. All we need do is find his year group and P level attained in 'Speaking' as shown on Table 6.1. The table shows that his year group is 3 and he scored 2.5 in 'Speaking'. A look at the graph for 'Speaking' (Figure 6.1) shows that there is a score of 2.5 for a Year 3 pupil, and that must be Alex Bigg's score. The score of 2.5 for Year 3 on the graph is below the grey band. Therefore, Alex Bigg's score of 2.5 in 'Speaking' is in the bottom 25% of the scores of similar pupils in the sample. The graph also shows that the score of 2.5 in 'Speaking' is also below the average score of Alex Bigg's year group in his school. In this way the scores of all the pupils can be identified on the graph to enable comparisons to be made.

Uses of the initial feedback

The initial feedback can be used by teachers to:

1. Compare the performances of pupils in different subjects. The attainment levels in 'Speaking' for SLD pupils are shown in

Figure 6.1. Similar graphs will be obtained for the attainment levels of SLD pupils in 'Listening', 'Reading', 'Writing', 'Using and applying', 'Number', 'Shapes, space and measures', and the strands of Science and PSHE. This enables the teacher to compare the P scales attainment levels of a pupil in different subjects in order to find their strong and weak points. There is a graph for each subject for pupils with each special need.

2. Compare the attainment levels of a pupil with similar pupils elsewhere. The grey band on the graph was derived from data collected on all SLD pupils in the sample. Therefore a comparison of a pupils' attainment level against the band implies a comparison with similar pupils in the whole sample.

3. Compare a pupil's attainment levels with similar pupils in their school. The initial feedback shows the attainment levels of pupils with the same special need in a school plotted against their year group. With the chart it is possible to compare the attainment levels of pupils in the same year group in the school by simply comparing the pupil's diamond with the joined diamond that corresponds to the average score of the pupil's year group.

4. Compare the attainment levels of any cohorts of our choice. It is possible to compare the average attainments of two or more cohorts in the sample. For example, we can choose to compare the average scores in any subjects of different year groups, different special needs or gender, etc.

Predictions

A table of predictions was introduced into the feedback in 2005 as a guide for teachers while setting improvement targets. The predictions were calculated using multiple regression techniques, taking into consideration the attainment levels of the current and previous years, the current age and the age of the pupils in the coming year. A typical table of predictions is shown in Table 6.2.

The table shows the names of pupils, their attainment levels in 'Reading' and 'Writing' in 2006 and the levels predicted for them for 2007. Abash Bettim with a score of P4 in 'Reading' in 2006 is expected to score 4.8 in 2007. Lisa Scotting who scored P2(i) in 2006 in 'Writing' is expected to score P2(ii) in 2007.

Table 6.2: Table of predicted levels for pupils (pseudonyms used)

Forename	Surname	Year group	Score in Reading in 2006	Predicted score in Reading for 2007	Score in Writing in 2006	Predicted score in Writing for 2007
Abash	Bettim	1	4	4.8	4	4.5
Aaron	Winty	1	5	5.5	4	4.5
Aisha	Monty	2	4	5	5	5.6
Charles	Kings	2	6	6.5	4	4.4
Kate	Claypath	3	5	5.5	4	4.4
Lange	Walsher	3	8	9	8	9
Lisa	Scotting	3	2	2.5	2	2.5
Melissa	Graines	4	6	6.7	6	6.5
Miranda	Kettly	5	8	8.5	7	7.3
Tim	Mannings	6	12	13	11	11.3
Todd	Lanchester	6	9	9.6	8	8.7

Percentiles

The table of percentiles was also introduced in 2005. A typical table of percentiles is shown in Table 6.3.

The table of percentiles presents an additional way of looking at the data. The percentile of a P scales attainment level gives the percentage of pupils in that category whose attainment levels are lower than that of the pupil who attained the level. Assuming that Table 6.3 is the percentile table for Year 6 MLD pupils, then Amy

Table 6.3: Table of percentiles (pseudonyms used)

Fore name	Last name	Reading	Percentiles for Reading	Number	Percentiles for Number
Amy	Aintree	12	94	11	93
Aisa	Jacobs	5	51	6	64
Greg	Tommy	9	84	9	81
Neil	Onyeisi	7	76	8	76
Tony	Grubber	8	78	9	81
Aishatu	Umaru	6	68	7	68
James	Okoro	7	76	8	76
Emily	Tamas	6	68	9	81

Aintree's score of 12 (L2c) in 'Reading' is on the 94th percentile. This puts her score in the top 6% of year group 6 MLD pupils for 'Reading'. Similarly, James Okoro's score of 8 (P8) which is equivalent to the 76th percentile puts his attainment in 'Number' within the top 24% of Year 6 MLD pupils, with 76% of scores in his year group in the whole sample falling below his.

Chances graphs

Chances graphs were another statistical device introduced in 2005. The chances graph is a distribution of the current scores of pupils who scored a given level in the previous year. A chances graph is shown below:

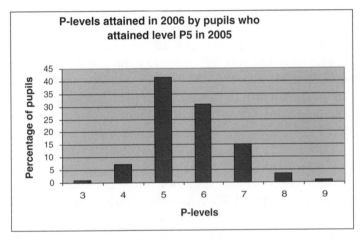

Figure 6.2: Chances graph.

The chances graph shows the distribution of 2006 attainment levels in 'Writing' for pupils who scored P5 in 'Writing' in 2005. The graph indicates that about 42% of the pupils who scored P5 in 2005 also scored P5 in 2006. About 32% of them scored P6 in 2006.

Value-added feedback

In general, the vast majority of pupils increase their level of academic achievement as they pass through school. Reading ages rise, vocabularies widen and an individual's mathematical knowledge grows. These increases in achievement can be regarded as progress.

The amount of progress over a certain period of time will naturally differ between individuals. If we looked at all pupils of a certain age and measured their progress over a certain period of time, we would find some pupils would make little progress, most pupils would make a near to average progress, and a few would make exceptional progress.

Most people would accept that, as well as being subject to natural variation, the improvements in achievement owe something to the environments in which pupils find themselves. The quality of teaching, availability of resources and many other factors may have a significant effect on the progress of individual pupils.

The progress that a pupil makes relative to that made by similar pupils in other schools can be identified as the 'value added' score for that pupil.

This measure is often referred to by experts as the residual because it is that which is left over after the pupil's starting point has been taken into account. The residual or value added score will be influenced by many factors such as effort, health, home experiences and help from others, in addition to the teaching and resources provided by the school. The residual will also be influenced by chance 'error' such as guessing, luck with item spotting, careless mistakes and so on. Nevertheless, the average residual (value added) is the best available indicator of the net effect a school has on the progress of a pupil. Therefore value added could be described as that additional progress the pupil makes which is the result of the effect the school has had on them and which the pupil would not have made had the school been unable to exert that influence.

Value added analysis of the P scales data

Value added analysis needs a starting point or baseline score and a final score for each pupil. The baseline score for the P scales project is taken to be the P scales attainment levels of the previous year. Therefore, value added scores can be calculated only for pupils whose achievements are recorded in two consecutive years.

Because of the very high correlations between the strands within each subject area, the value added scores for the P scales is usually calculated using the average scores of strands of each subject area. Hence, for the purpose of value added calculations, Literacy is the average of 'Speaking', 'Listening', 'Speaking and Listening', 'Reading' and 'Writing'. Similarly Numeracy is the average of 'Using and applying', 'Number' and 'Shape, space and measures', whilst Science is the average of 'Scientific enquiry', 'Life processes', 'Materials and their properties' and 'Physical processes'.

There is one value added table for each principal need and so schools receive as many tables as the number of principal needs they have in the data. A typical value added feedback table is shown in Table 6.4. For Literacy, Numeracy and Science the table shows the average scores in 2006 and 2007, the predicted score and the value added for each pupil. The predicted score in this context refers to the level the pupil is expected to score based on their previous and current score.

The value added score is standardised to have a mean of 100 and a standard deviation of 1. Value added below 100 mean that the pupil achieved less than expected for pupils of similar ability. Value added above 100 mean that a pupil achieved higher than expected for pupils of the same ability. A value added score that is exactly 100 means that the pupil achieved the expected score for pupils of similar ability.

In Table 6.4, the pupils Jenny Bott and Alexander Kridge have value added higher than 100 in both Literacy and Numeracy. This shows that in 2007 these pupils achieved above the expectations for pupils of similar ability in Year 8 in both Literacy and Numeracy.

On the other hand, Jack Orange and Zainab Kash have value added lower than 100 in both subject areas and have therefore achieved lower than expected for pupils of similar ability in Years 9 and 10 respectively. Harry Dean has achieved above expectations in Literacy but below expectations in Numeracy.

The ranking of pupils' value added data

The value added cells for each pupil have been coded with shading according to the value added scores and how highly the pupil's progress ranks among the progress made by pupils of same year group, principal need and prior attainment. For example, using the

Table 6.4: Value added table (pseudonyms used)

Name and Year group			Literacy				Numeracy			
First name	Last name	Year Group	Average Score in 2006	Average Score in 2007	Predicted Score	Value Added for Literacy	Average Score in 2006	Average Score in 2007	Predicted Score	Value Added for Numeracy
Jenny	Bott	8	8.7	12.3	9.1	102.32	8	10	8.6	100.89
Alex	Kridge	8	11.3	12.7	11.7	101.82	10	11.5	10.4	102.45
Jack	Orange	9	16	16	16.3	99.51	15.5	15.5	15.7	99.59
Garry	Apples	9	11.3	11	11.7	98.79	12.3	12.8	12.6	100.43
Jerry	Winger	9	7.3	8.3	7.8	100.94	8.5	8	8.9	97.93
Zainab	Kash	10	14	14	14.3	99.43	15	15	15.2	99.55
Shara	Kenba	10	11.7	12.3	12.1	100.41	13	14	13.3	101.59
Harry	Dean	10	10.3	12.7	10.5	102.42	16	15	16.4	99.02
Renny	Watkins	10	11.7	13.3	11.9	101.55	9	13	9.4	102.45
Jenny	Okoro	10	12.7	11.7	12.9	98.66	9	9	9.4	99.7
Lemarry	Binns	10	13	12	13.2	98.67	15	15	15.4	99.71

top 2.5% | top 16% | middle 68% | bottom 16% | bottom 2.5%

shading it is possible to say whether pupil A's progress in a particular subject is in the top 2.5% or bottom 2.5% of the progress made by pupils of the same year group, principal need and prior attainment. The example of the patterns is shown below.

Increasing progress above average   Decreasing progress below

| 1 | 2 | 3 | 4 | 5 |

(boxes: top 2.5%, top 16%, middle 68%, bottom 16%, bottom 2.5%)

If a pupil has their value added coded with horizontal stripes as in box 1 of the illustration above, then their value added is within the top 2.5% of the value-added of all pupils in the sample with the same year group, principal need and prior attainment. If a pupil has their value added shaded light gray as in box 5, then their value added is in the lowest 2.5% of the value added of all pupils in the sample with the same year group, principal need and prior attainment as them. Other patterns can be interpreted in a similar way. Value added scores shaded with horizontal stripes mean excellent progress and a value added shaded light gray signals concern.

Teachers can use the P scales value added feedback to study:

- the progress of each pupil in different subjects. The value added is calculated for each subject area and because it is standardised teachers can compare each pupil's value added in any two of English, Mathematics or Science.
- the progress of similar pupils. Teachers can compare the value added of similar pupils, (i.e pupils of same year and principal need who attained the same P level in the previous year) to establish who has made more progress.
- The year-on-year progress of each pupil in each subject. A record of year-on-year value added of each pupil will enable teachers to keep track of pupils' year-on-year progress.

The P scales data collection exercise and the resulting feedback have been seen as very useful to schools as expressed in the following comments taken from many sent in by headteachers.

- 'The feedback has assisted the school in setting objective-led targets and assessing progress for children in the Early Years Reception class and Year 1/Year 2 class.'
- 'The school has been using the levels extensively since their initial publication and CEM data (the feedback) greatly helps in the continuing evaluation of their use and the school's progress.'
- 'Participation in the QCA P scales data collection project at Durham University has been extremely useful in monitoring the efficacy of all teaching and learning at our school. It furnishes us with tangible evidence of individual pupil progression, assists in the setting of realistic targets for cohorts of pupils with similar needs across the various phases of education, and, crucially, enables us to measure performance within curriculum areas and strands.'

General Trends Observed during the Analysis of P scales Data since 1999

Over the years the P scales datasets collected annually have been subjected to general statistical analysis to search for trends. Several have been identified. Variations have been examined in (1) the number of schools in the project each year since 1999; (2) the percentages of special and mainstream schools in the project; (3) the percentages of boys and girls in the project; and (4) the distribution of pupils across the categories of Special Educational Needs over the years. These are presented below. The average attainments of PMLD, SLD and MLD in the cognitive as well as PSHE scales are also presented.

The number of schools in the project each year

The variation of the number of schools in the project since 1999 is shown in Figure 6.3.

The total number of schools in the project fell from 1029 in 2004 to 500 in 2005 after QCA withdrew their sponsorship resulting in schools being required to pay for participation in the project.

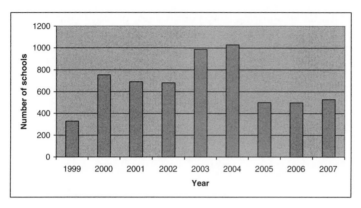

Figure 6.3: School participation in the P scales data collection project each year from 1999 to 2007.

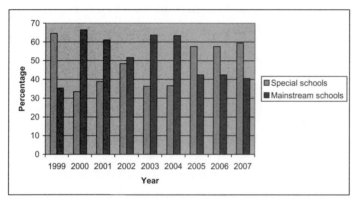

Figure 6.4: Distribution of special and mainstream schools in the P scales data collection project from 1999 to 2007.

The percentages of special and mainstream schools

In 2005, 2006 and 2007 the total number of schools and the percentages of special and mainstream schools in the project remained almost the same (Figure 6.4). In 2007 there were 528 schools and 25,242 pupils in the project compared with 498 schools and 22,972 pupils in 2006.

Until 2004, with the exception of 1999 and 2002, the percentages of special and mainstream schools taking part in the P scales were

Table 6.5: Table showing the percentages of boys and girls in the P scales data collection project from 1999 to 2007

Year	Boys in sample (%)	Girls in sample (%)
1999	64.9	35.1
2000	75.7	24.3
2001	66.3	33.7
2002	67.0	33.0
2003	68.0	32.0
2004	68.0	32.0
2005	67.0	33.0
2006	67.4	32.6
2007	63.9	36.1

fairly consistent. The data collection was first conducted in 1999 and most schools in the project for that year were special schools because at that time most mainstream schools were unaware that the P scales were applicable to some of their pupils.

The percentages of boys and girls in the project

The percentages of boys and girls in the data collection exercise remained nearly constant from 1999 to 2006 apart from the year 2000 (Table 6.5). It is remarkable that this trend persisted despite the significant variations in the total number of pupils each year.

The distribution of pupils across the categories of Special Educational Need

The distribution of pupils across Special Educational Needs in the P scales data collected in 2001, 2002 and 2003 respectively is shown in Figure 6.5.

It is clear from Figure 6.5 that MLD and SLD dominated in terms of pupil numbers, and again it is remarkable that the same trend persisted in the distribution of pupils across the special needs categories for the three years. The distribution of special needs in different authorities was also found to be similar.

Comparison of achievement scores for pupils having PMLD, SLD and MLD

Achievement scores were derived by obtaining the means of all the cognitive scales (cognitive scales refer to all subject areas apart from PSHE). This was justified by the very high correlations between the cognitive scales. The distributions of pupils across the achievement scores for the three categories of learning difficulty are shown in Figures 6.6, 6.7, and 6.8. In Figure 6.6 the distribution for PMLD

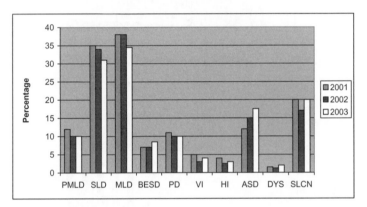

Figure 6.5: Distribution of pupils across special educational need in the P scales data collection project in 2001, 2002 and 2003.

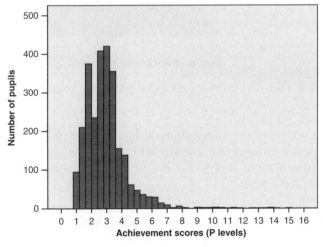

Figure 6.6: Distribution of achievement scores for Year 9 PMLD pupils.

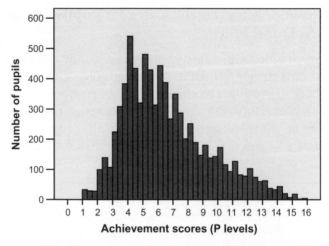

Figure 6.7: Distribution of achievement scores for Year 9 SLD pupils.

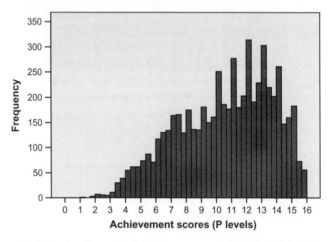

Figure 6.8: Distribution of achievement scores for Year 9 MLD pupils.

pupils is, as expected, skewed towards the lower P levels. The histogram peaks around the score of P3.

In Figure 6.7 the scores for the SLD pupils range from P2 to about L4 of the National Curriculum, with the histogram peaking around P5.

In Figure 6.8, the distribution for MLD pupils is clearly skewed to the right of the histogram towards the high scores.

On average MLD pupils scored higher than SLD, who on average scored higher than PMLD. The modes for the distributions of achievement scores for PMLD, SLD and MLD were 2, 4, and 12 respectively.

Comparison of average attainments for PMLD, SLD and MLD pupils

Figures 6.9 and 6.10 show the average P scales scores in 'Reading' and 'Scientific enquiry' for the three learning difficulty classifications by year group.

As with the National Curriculum levels, it was expected that pupils would show progress through the P scales with age. Figures 6.9 and 6.10 show that from primary school to the end of compulsory schooling, both MLD and SLD students made progress through the P scales. However, there was little progress recorded for PMLD pupils, perhaps because maintaining present competences is a major achievement for some pupils. These two examples are typical of the graphs for all the cognitive P scales, which clearly showed very similar growth patterns. Indeed, the pattern shown in

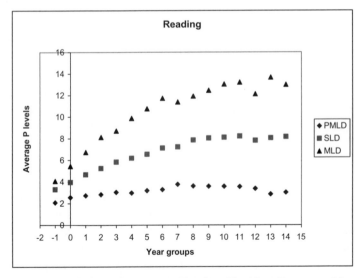

Figure 6.9: Average P scale score in 'Reading' by Year Group and learning difficulty classification.

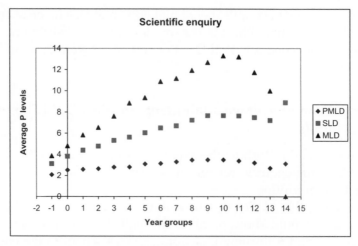

Figure 6.10: Average P scale score in 'Scientific enquiry' by Year Group and learning difficulty classification.

these graphs repeated itself for the Personal, Social and Health Education (PSHE) scale (Figure 6.11). *Similar trends were observed in the data sets collected in all years of the data collection and analysis.*

Figure 6.11 shows the average PSHE scores for the three learning difficulty classifications (PMLD, SLD and MLD) by year group. Once again, through the years from primary school to the end of compulsory schooling, both MLD and SLD students were recorded as making progress, whilst less progress was recorded for PMLD pupils. It is interesting to note, however, that the most rapid progress for all groups appeared to be in the years up to Year 6. These trends have been consistent throughout the years the P scales data have been collected and confirm that the average attainments of the three learning difficulty categories are in the order MLD > SLD > PMLD.

Although in Figures 6.9–6.11 for each year group the average scores for the learning difficulty categories seem to be clearly different, the box plot diagram shown in Figure 6.12 shows that the distributions of the actual scores do overlap. Therefore the attainment level cannot be used in the identification of a pupil's learning difficulty. Figure 6.12 shows that there is a drop in achievement after Year 10 for MLD pupils. This drop occurs because more able pupils move on to other things after Year 10.

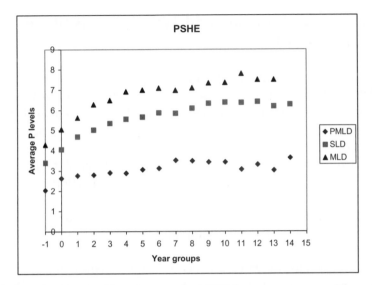

Figure 6.11: Average P scale score in PSHE by year group and learning difficulty classification.

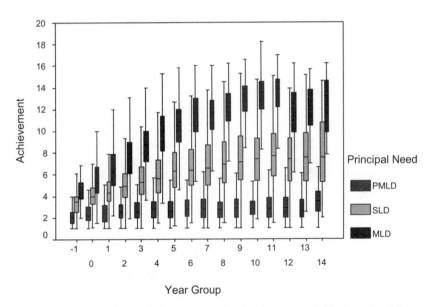

Figure 6.12: Average achievement score by learning difficulty classification and year group. Note: The achievement score was calculated as the average of the 12 cognitive P scales.

The P scales Software and What Schools Stand to Gain from It

Software has been included annually since 2007 as an additional feedback item for schools subscribing to the Durham P scales data analysis. Its addition was in response to the continuous call from teachers for software that would enable them to examine their P scales data from different perspectives.

During school inspections, evidence is gathered to ascertain whether a school is performing well. This inspection is usually carried out by inspectors from the Office for Standards in Education (Ofsted). Although there are several aspects to a school inspection, the examination of the attainment and progress of pupils is a very important part of the process.

Apart from the information a school enters on the Self-Evaluation Form (SEF) supplied by Ofsted, it is required to provide evidence about pupils' learning. The school is expected to present an accurate record for each child, showing their attainments as they enter the school and their progress as they pass through the key stages. Therefore a system that tracks a pupil's journey as they enter and progress through the school is one of the sources of evidence that Ofsted inspectors expect schools to present during inspection.

Although the information required by schools to conduct school and pupil evaluation is contained in the initial and value-added feedback packages, schools are required to extract information from these feedback packages and put them into the form required by the inspectors. Most schools have no problem extracting and presenting their data, but some teachers find it very demanding. The P scales software has been prepared so that schools can examine their data from different perspectives and present that data to inspectors automatically without any additional work.

Description of the P scales software

The P scales software is built on the Microsoft Excel software. The implication is that each school has their data on one Excel worksheet without the encumbrance of an external database. This ensures that schools can copy and save their copy of the software to any folder they choose without generating any errors. However, in order to run the software, each school must have Microsoft Excel

1997 or later installed. In addition, schools must ensure that their PC or laptop has been set up to run macros, if not their IT manager should be consulted.

Functions built into the software enable schools to:

- Graphically compare the attainment levels of individual pupils in all subjects in the current year.
- Keep track of the attainment levels of individual pupils over the number of years that they have participated in the Durham P scales project.
- Graphically compare the average scores by age group and gender.
- Graphically compare their pupils' attainment levels in all subjects with those of the whole sample.
- Graphically examine the percentage of their pupils that have made above average progress in English, Mathematics and Science in the past year.
- Graphically examine the percentages of their pupils that have progressed by at least one P level compared to the whole sample.
- Access the predicted scores for their pupils.
- Use the software to check whether in the current year their pupils have actually attained the levels that were predicted for them.

Schools that participated in the previous year with some or all of the pupils also in the project in the current year can use the software to:

- Graphically compare the value added for each pupil in the three core subject areas of English, Mathematics and Science for the current year.
- Monitor the progress of each pupil by tracking their value added in the three core subject areas of English, Mathematics and Science over the period they have been in the Durham P scales project.
- Calculate the value added for any additional pupil they may have.
- Compare the value added for boys and girls.

Starting

The P scales software is available on the CEM, Durham University secure server over the internet. Participating schools download the software using the username and password they have been sent

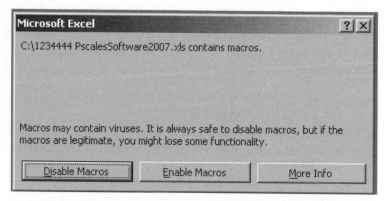

Figure 6.13: Click on Enable macros to open your software.

from CEM and each school has their own school-specific version of the software available to them. Hence the software is appropriately named 'XXXXXXX Pscales YYYY Software.xls' where XXXXXXX is the school's DCSF number and YYYY the year of the project. On double clicking the software file the dialog box shown in Figure 6.13 will be displayed:

Click on **Enable Macros** to open the software which you should now save to any folder of your choice on your PC or laptop. Please ensure you save it on your computer before you open it for use and remember to click on **Enable macros** each time you want to open it.

Choosing the right functions for the right job

If your computer runs macros, on opening, the software exposes the five combo boxes, Box 1, Box 2, Box 3, Box 4 and Box 5. All functions are contained in the boxes and by clicking on the arrows to the right-hand side of each box, a list of the functions of each will be revealed.

Descriptions of the software functions and how to access them

Comparing each pupil's attainment in all subjects
Schools often need to compare the performances of a pupil in different subject areas. The need could arise either during school

inspection or for feedback to parents or guardians. Schools can readily access this information using the P scales software.

Box 1 appears on the left-hand corner of your screen (see Figure 6.14). Figure 6.15(a) shows data accessed by clicking on the arrow to the right-hand side of Box 1.

Go to Box 1 and select the function called 'Current Year's data'. This action will reveal the names of all the pupils in the school's

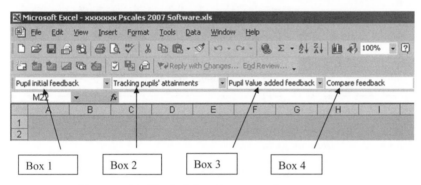

Figure 6.14: Top left-hand corner of your screen.

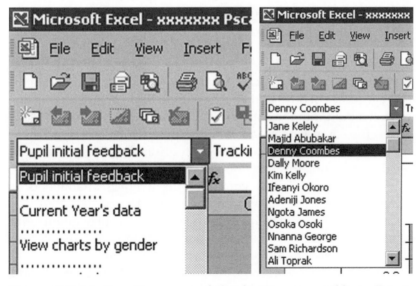

Figure 6.15 (a): Revealing some of the functions accessible in Box 1. **(b):** Revealing pupils' names.

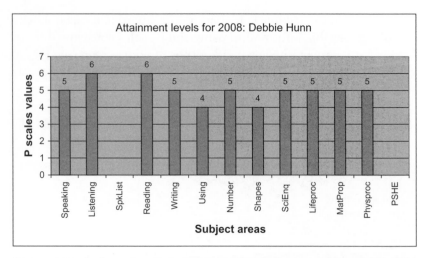

Figure 6.16: A chart showing attainment levels for a pupil named Debbie Hunn. Using this chart it is possible to see how she has performed in different subject areas in 2008.

current year data (see Figure 6.15(b)). If you then scroll down and select the name of any pupil of your choice from the list, their attainment levels in all the subjects in the current year will be displayed, as shown in Figure 6.16.

Comparing average attainment levels of boys and girls
Several schools have indicated that they would like to compare the average scores of boys in their school with those of girls. A function has been built into the software to enable schools to automatically access the comparative data when required. This can be accessed from Box 1 when the user selects the function 'View charts by gender'. Selecting this function reveals a chart similar to that shown in Figure 6.17(a), which compares the average attainments in 'Scientific enquiry' by year group and gender.

The chart shows that the differences in the average attainments of boys and girls differed for most of the year groups. However, the differences were not tested for statistical significance.

Users can compare average attainments in any subject by clicking on that subject in the panel provided at the right-hand side of the chart. Figure 6.17(b) shows some of the subjects displayed on the panel.

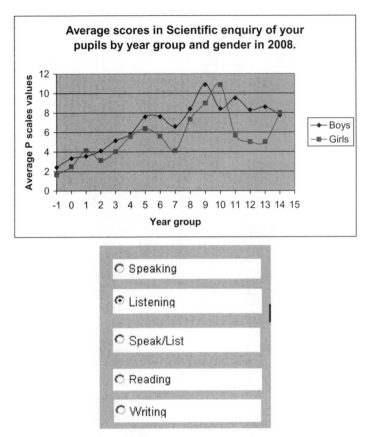

Figure 6.17 (a): Chart showing the average attainments in 'Scientific enquiry' by year group and gender. **(b):** Subjects.

Tracking each pupil's attainments over a period of time
Tracking a pupil's performances or monitoring a pupil's attainment levels is vital. It provides the information inspectors must consider when they are at a school. To track the attainment levels of a pupil over a few years, go to Box 2 and select the function named 'Track pupils'. This action loads the names of the pupils for whom you have returned P scales data since 2005. Scrolling downwards on Box 2 and selecting a pupil from the pupil list will reveal a chart displaying the data available for that pupil. The chart displays the attainment levels for the pupil in each subject for the years the pupil has been in the P scales project since 2005. There is a set of graphs for each child, and an example chart is shown in Figure 6.18.

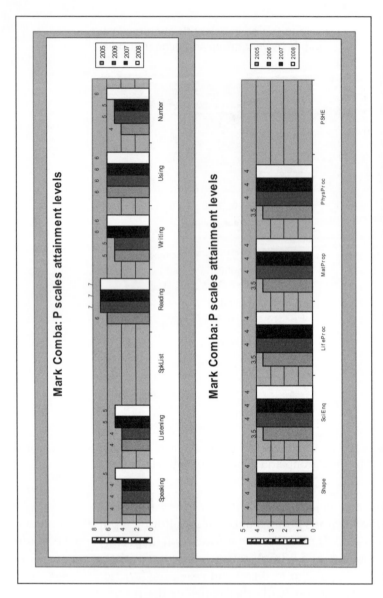

Figure 6.18: The chart shows the attainments of a pupil named Mark Comba in several subjects over a period of four years.

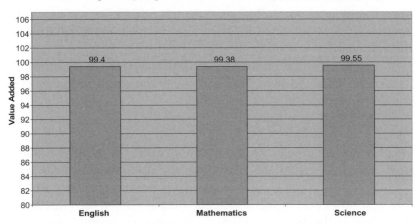

Figure 6.19: Value added for a pupil named Denisa Kings.

The chart shows that while the pupil has progressed in some subjects his attainment has remained the same in others.

Accessing the value added for each pupil
To view the value added of each pupil in the three core subject areas for the current year, go to Box 3 and select the function named 'Value Added for YYYY' where YYYY is the year the software was issued. This will cause the names of all pupils in your school that have value added scores for the current year to be entered in the box. The chart will display the value added for any pupil whose name you select from the list. Figure 6.19 shows the value added in English, Mathematics and Science for a pupil named Denisa Kings.

The value added here has been standardised to have a mean of 100 and a standard deviation of 1. A value added of 100 shows the pupil has made average progress compared to similar pupils in the sample. A value added above 100 shows that the pupil has made above average progress and a value added below 100 shows that the pupil has made below average progress.

Calculating value added

There may be a pupil not entered for the project for one reason or another. The value added for such a pupil can be calculated using the value-added wizard built into the software.

To calculate value added, go to Box 3 and select the function 'Calculate Value Added'. This will cause the value-added wizard shown in Figure 6.20 to be displayed.

As seen in Figure 6.20, there are tabs for English, Mathematics and Science. Click on the appropriate tab to select the subject for which you wish to calculate value added. Enter the pupil's principal need and year group. Then enter in the appropriate boxes their average scores in the subject area of your interest for last year and this year and click on the 'Calculate' button. The value added will be given in the box provided. To convert the pupil's scores to numbers before calculating averages, please use the re-coding criteria on page 6 of the document titled *P scales Feedback Booklet 2008*.

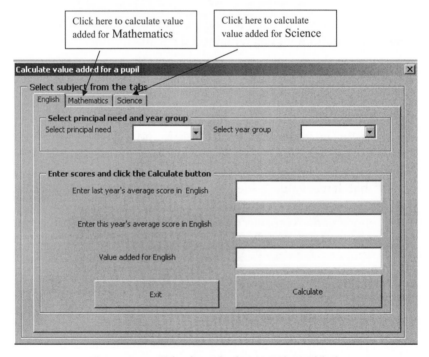

Figure 6.20: Tabs for calculating value added.

You will find this booklet in the 'Downloads' menu on the website where you access your feedback.

Comparing value added for boys and girls
If you want to compare the value added for boys and girls in your school go to Box 3 and select the function 'Compare boys and girls'. You will see a chart similar to Figure 6.21 below.

Figure 6.21 shows the average value added for boys and girls for English, Mathematics and Science. The chart shows that, on average, over the past year girls made more progress than boys in English and Science. On the other hand, over the same period, boys made more progress than girls in Mathematics.

Accessing the percentage of pupils in your school that made above average progress
If you want to find out the percentage of pupils in your school that have made above average progress, then select the option 'Pupils that progressed' in Box 4. This action will reveal a chart displaying the percentage of pupils in your school that have made above average progress in each subject area on which you have sent data.

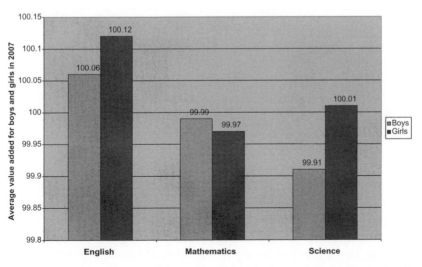

Figure 6.21: Comparison of the value added for boys and girls in a school.

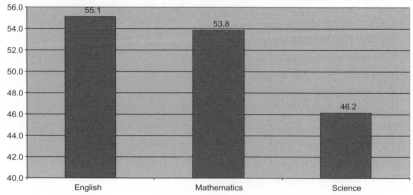

Figure 6.22: Chart showing the percentage of MLD pupils in the school that have made above average progress in each of the three subject areas.

Comparing the average attainment of pupils in a school with those of the whole sample

Headteachers have always wanted a facility that would enable them to compare the performances of their school with those of other schools. In response to this the P scales software has been equipped with a function that enables schools to compare the average attainment of their pupils with those of other pupils of similar age and special need. The software allows comparisons to be made in three subject areas, English, Mathematics and Science. To view this information, go to Box 4 and select the function 'Compare initial feedback'. This action will reveal Figure 6.23.

Check the special need category you wish to compare and click on the 'Proceed' button to be presented with a chart similar to that shown in Figure 6.24 if you have any pupils in that special need category. You will have a chart for each subject area in which you have data.

Figure 6.24 shows that the average score in English of Year 2 pupils in the school is higher than that of Year 2 pupils in the whole sample. Year 1 and Years 3–14 in the school have lower average scores in English than the corresponding year groups in the whole sample. On the other hand, the reception pupils (Year 0) in the school and those in the whole sample have same average scores in English.

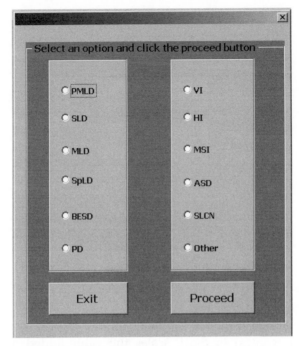

Figure 6.23: Special need options to choose from.

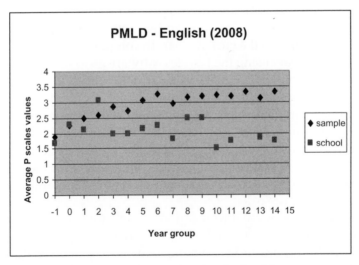

Figure 6.24: Comparing average P levels of school by year group with those of whole sample.

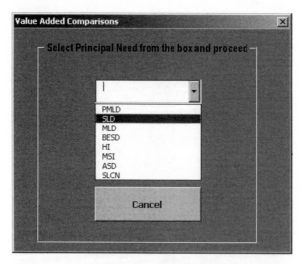

Figure 6.25: Choose principal need from the box.

Tracking pupils' progress over the years
The value-added feedback is a measure of a pupil's relative progress. In the context of the P scales the value added measures a pupil's progress based on their prior attainment, age and special need category. Schools need the ability to readily access records showing pupils' progress over the years. Using the P scales software you can compare the progress a pupil made in a subject area in the previous year (value added) with their progress in the same subject area in the current year. To compare a pupil's progress over several years using the P scales software go to Box 4 and select the function named 'Compare value added'. This will present you with the dialog box shown in Figure 6.25.

On the combo box select the principal need of the pupils whose progress (value added) you want to compare and click on the proceed button to enter the names of the pupils. Select a pupil's name to view a chart comparing their value added for the number of years they have been on the project. A typical comparison graph is shown in Figure 6.26.

Figure 6.26 shows that Kim Tarino made below average progress in English in 2005, 2006 and 2008, but above average progress in 2007. Kim's progress in Mathematics and Science followed the same trend. Kim made greater progress in all subjects in 2007. In fact,

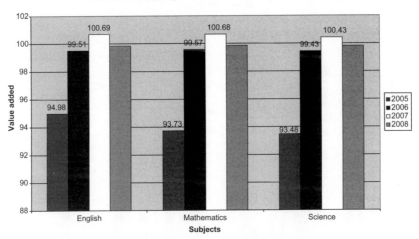

Figure 6.26: Comparison of yearly value added of a pupil.

Kim's progress in all three subjects in 2007 was above average. However, in 2008 her progress was below average. Since it is clear from the chart that Kim's progress in all three subject areas was continuous from 2005 to 2007 before a dip in 2008, it is necessary to check whether there has been any change in Kim's circumstances since the end of the 2007 academic year.

Retrieving information on pupils that progressed by at least 1 P level
School inspectors often want to know what percentage of pupils in a year group has made progress and such information should be readily available. Therefore, this information is stored in the software and updated each year. The information is stored in the software in such a way that it enables users to compare the percentage of their pupils that have made progress in their school with those in the whole sample. If you want to view a chart showing the percentage of your pupils that have progressed by at least one P level over the past year go to Box 4 and select the function named 'P level progress'. This will show you a chart similar to that in Figure 6.27.

Figure 6.27 shows that 21.6% of all pupils in the school progressed in 'Speaking' by at least one P level in the past year while 30.9% of pupils in the sample made similar progress. Figure 6.27

Percentages of pupils that progressed by at least 1 P level in each subject in 2008 compared with the whole sample.

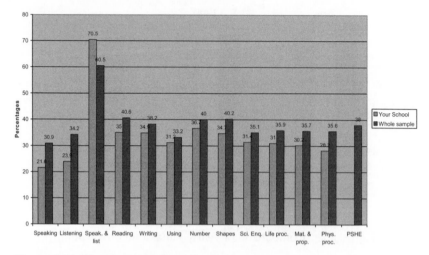

Figure 6.27: Percentages of pupils that have progressed by at least one P level over the past year. Percentages for the whole sample are also shown in the same chart for comparison.

also shows that 35% and 36.7% of pupils in the school progressed by at least one P level in 'Reading' and 'Number' respectively, whilst 40.6% and 40% of the sample made similar progress. It is apparent that a higher percentage of pupils in the sample progressed by at least one P level compared to the percentage of pupils that progressed within the school.

Retrieving information on predicted and attained scores of pupils
One of the reasons for which the P scales project at Durham University was initially established in 1999 and financially supported by the DCSF was to provide schools with data that would enable them to set improvement targets for their pupils. Therefore, predicted attainment levels for the coming year are part of the feedback that schools receive. The P scales software contains a function that enables teachers to readily verify at the end of the academic year whether or not a pupil has attained the target set for them at the beginning of the year. In order to compare a pupil's current attainment with their target, go to Box 4 and select 'Targets and attainments'. This will reveal a sheet showing the predicted

scores. Against each predicted score field you will see a corresponding score if any score has been entered for the pupil this year. Green cells show that the attained level is higher than that predicted. The blue level shows that the predicted and attained levels are equal, while yellow cells indicate that the attained level is lower than the predicted level.

Accessing predicted scores for your pupils for next year
If you want to view the levels that each pupil is predicted to attain in various subjects in 2009 then go to Box 4 and select 'Predictions'. This will reveal a sheet showing the predicted scores. Please remember that the predicted scores are for next year.

Comparing the value added of your school with those of the sample
If you want to see how the value added for your school compares with that of the whole sample then go to Box 5. In Box 5 select the option 'Compare school progress with sample'. You will be shown a dialog box having a combo box from which you can select a principal need. After selecting a principal need from the combo click on the 'Proceed' key and you will see a chart similar to that shown in Figure 6.28.

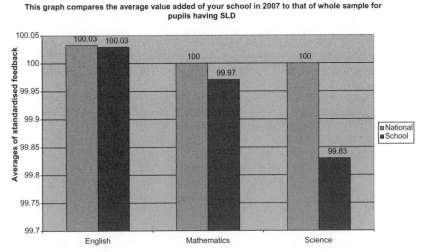

Figure 6.28: Average value added of whole school compared to average value added of whole sample.

Should pupils' attainment and progress (value added) be presented according to Special Educational Need category?

Some teachers have suggested that the presentation of attainment and progress data for pupils with Special Educational Needs should not involve their Special Educational Needs categories. In fact, Ofsted has advised that schools should take into account only age and prior attainment when calculating the attainments and progress of these pupils.

To date we are not aware of any empirical evidence in support of the call to ignore special educational categories when presenting pupils' attainments and progress. It is not clear why age and prior attainment were highlighted as the only factors to be considered whilst ignoring others such as special need, gender, ethnicity, social background, etc. Where is the evidence that pupils' attainments and progress will change with age no matter their special need, social background, ethnicity, or gender?

At the Centre for Evaluation and Monitoring (CEM) at Durham University, the feedback from the annual P scales data collection, which includes comparison of attainments, value added, predictions of future attainments, percentiles, etc., have, since 2000, been calculated and presented according to the special needs of pupils.

In this section we present evidence from the results of the analysis of P scales data collected from 522 schools and 24,357 pupils in 2008. The evidence proves that special need is too important a factor to be ignored when the attainments and progress of pupils with SEN are being calculated.

It was clearly demonstrated in Figures 6.9–6.12 that attainments by pupils with learning difficulties depended on the severity of the learning difficulty. Hence, average attainments by year group for pupils with PMLD, SLD and MLD were in the order MLD > SLD > PMLD. The same trend was also observed in PSHE. It was also clear from Figures 6.9–6.12 that PMLD pupils did not make any quantifiable progress. Thus, the special needs category of a pupil affected their attainment levels and must be considered as an important factor in the calculation and presentation of attainment and progress data. The value added (relative progress) of a pupil is basically what is left after their expected score is subtracted from their actual score. In order to examine the effect of combining pupils of different learning difficulties in one cohort during the calculation of their relative progress, expected scores were calculated separately for PMLD, SLD and MLD pupils and repeated when all the pupils were combined in one cohort. The calculations were carried out for each year group using an assumed prior attainment. The analysis was also carried out for the special need categories BESD, PD, VI, HI and SLCN.

In Table 6.6, the columns named 'PMLD', 'SLD' and 'MLD' contain the expected scores and value added when the pupils had their special need categories taken into account during calculations. The column 'Learning difficulty ignored' has the expected scores when the calculations were carried out with all the pupils merged into one cohort ignoring their learning difficulty categories.

Table 6.6 shows that for each year group, the expected scores for the three learning difficulty categories increased with decreasing severity of the learning difficulty despite the fact that the prior attainment was the same. In other words, the expected scores are in the order of MLD > SLD > PMLD. This is just as teachers would

Table 6.6: Expected scores for pupils classified as PMLD, SLD and MLD, with prior attainment of P3(i) in Mathematics, by year group

Year group	PMLD Expected score	SLD Expected score	MLD Expected score	Learning difficulty ignored Expected score
2	3.2	3.5	4.1	3.5
3	3.1	3.4	4.1	3.4
4	3.1	3.5	4.2	3.4
5	3.1	3.3	3.9	3.3
6	3.2	3.4	4.3	3.4
7	3.0	3.5	4.2	3.3
8	3.1	3.4	4.5	3.4
9	3.0	3.4	4.9	3.4
10	3.1	3.5	4.7	3.6
11	3.0	3.3	4.9	3.3
12	3.1	3.3	3.9	3.3
13	3.0	3.6	4.1	3.3
14	3.1	3.7	4.4	3.3

anticipate because higher attainments are expected from pupils with less severe conditions. Further, Table 6.6 shows that for the same prior attainment, if a PMLD pupil has their special need ignored, their expected score is higher than when it is not ignored. On the other hand, an MLD pupil with the same prior attainment had lower expected scores when they were in the same cohort with pupils of PMLD and SLD. Because value added (relative progress) is what is left after the expected score is subtracted from the current score, the PMLD child will have a lower value added (relative progress) when they are in a cohort with SLD and MLD pupils than when they are not. The opposite is true for the MLD child. They (MLD children) will have their value added enhanced when they are in a cohort with PMLD and SLD pupils.

This shows that ignoring pupils' special need category when calculating their value added (relative progress) introduces bias. Ignoring the learning difficulty category erroneously reduces the value added for some learning difficulty categories, for example PMLD, and enhances the value added for others, for example MLD.

Although the Special Educational Need categories HI, VI, PD, BESD and SLCN are not mutually exclusive, a graph of average attainments against year groups, Figure 6.29, shows a trend of

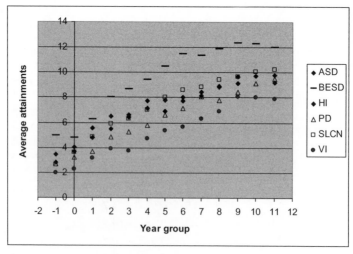

Figure 6.29: Average attainments of the Special Educational Needs categories ASD, BESD, HI, PD, SLCN and VI.

increasing average attainment with age. The graph also indicates that some of the special need categories have higher achievers than others. The average attainments are largely in the order, BESD > SLCN > PD > VI.

The higher achieving groups BESD and SLCN have their expected scores reduced when their special need categories were ignored as can be seen in Table 6.7. The high achieving groups, for example BESD and SLCN would have their value added enhanced if their special needs category was ignored. It is also clear that the low achieving groups, for example VI, PD and HI would be given inappropriately low value added scores if their category was disregarded.

Clearly, ignoring the special need categories of pupils during the calculation of their value added (relative progress) gives rise to erroneous results. When all pupils of different special need categories are gathered into one cohort the value added of the scores of relatively high achieving special need groups are enhanced, whilst those of the relatively low achieving groups are reduced. The value

Table 6.7: Expected scores by year group and special need categories for pupils with prior attainment of P3(i) in English

Year group	HI Expected score	VI Expected score	PD Expected score	BESD Expected score	SLCN Expected score	Special needs ignored Expected score
1	3.2	3.2	3.4	3.3	3.5	3.6
2	3.3	3.4	3.6	4.1	3.7	3.5
3	3.4	3.1	3.3	3.3	3.4	3.4
4	3.4	3.3	3.3	3.5	3.4	3.6
5	3.3	3.3	3.4	3.9	3.6	3.5
6	3.1	3.1	3.4	3.9	3.9	3.5
7	3.3	3.1	3.4	3.9	3.8	3.6
8	3.1	3.2	3.5	4.4	3.6	3.6
9	3.4	3.5	3.5	4.0	3.7	3.6
10	3.3	3.3	3.6	3.9	4.0	3.5
11	3.4	3.1	3.3	3.9	3.7	3.5

added of pupils of a given age, prior attainment and special need who made below average progress could erroneously increase to above average progress when the pupils are put in the same cohort with other pupils who may be low achieving. On the other hand, pupils of a special need category could have their value added reduced to below average if it is calculated in the same cohort with pupils of a different special need category who may be high achieving.

The presentation of attainments and progress of pupils with Special Educational Needs must take their special need category into account.

CHAPTER 7

Ways Forward

Francis Ndaji and Peter Tymms

Although use of the P scales is widespread among special (and even mainstream) schools they are not without criticism. Some of the criticisms have led to amendments and consequent improvements and the assessment criteria are still evolving. The P scales have competition from other systems of assessment for pupils working below Level 1 of the National Curriculum. Systems such as PIVATS and B Squared that are based on the P scales have emerged as competitors. This chapter outlines the criticisms of the P scales and the responses to those criticisms. Later it compares the P scales with the competing alternatives and highlights the merits and demerits of objective measures and teacher ratings.

The P scales assessment criteria are relatively new, and are still evolving. Some of the criticisms of the P scales are as follows:

- Some schools reported that there were too many tasks for their pupils to accomplish within each P level, with the result that it took pupils too long to complete one level and move to the next; some commented that pupils found it difficult to progress from one level to the next. As a result, they felt that progress made by some pupils, especially those with more serious needs, was difficult to detect.

The P scales: Assessing the Progress of Children with Special Educational Needs
Written and edited by Francis Ndaji and Peter Tymms
Copyright © 2009 John Wiley & Sons Ltd.

In response to this and other criticisms the P scales assessment criteria was reviewed in 2001. Specifically the level descriptors for P1, P2 and P3 were each split into two in order to make the system more sensitive at these low levels of cognition.

- Some schools were unhappy that there was little information on how best to assess pupils using the P scales. They thought there should be a standard procedure adhered to by everyone. They reported that the absence of a standard procedure gave rise to inconsistencies in the award of levels. For example, it became clear from interaction with the schools that whilst some schools awarded a P level to a pupil if that pupil had completed all the elements of that level, others awarded a level to a pupil if they could perform some of the elements of the level. The procedures adopted varied between schools. The overall effect of this was inconsistency in the data collected using the system. The inconsistency extended to problems within schools. In some schools procedures may have varied from one teacher to another. Some schools reported cases of the same pupil being awarded different levels on a subject by two teachers, or cases of a teacher awarding pupils levels that fell very far below or above the level awarded by another teacher in the previous year.

In response to the above criticism the QCA, in 2004, organised moderation sessions in selected cities in England. However, some schools still worry about the absence of standard procedures for assessing pupils when using the P scales.

- Although the P scales data collection and analysis have been successful as attested to by schools, there were suggestions by teachers a few years ago that a bottleneck existed between level P8 of the P scales and Level 1 of the National Curriculum. This suggestion arose as a result of the observation by the teachers that some of their pupils apparently found it very difficult to progress from P8 of the P scales to the next level which is Level 1c of the National Curriculum. However, this has been investigated at Durham University using both a classical approach and an Item Response Theory (IRT) method of analysis. The results of the analyses showed that no such bottleneck existed between

P8 and L1c in any subject. In fact no bottleneck was found between any two levels of the P scales.

- The maximum level for PSHE in the current version of the P scales is P8 (8) unlike in the earlier versions where the maximum score was 15. Some schools were unhappy that pupils could not be assessed on PSHE using a scale that went above P8. The schools were mostly those with many pupils categorised as having BESD who need to monitor changes in the behavioural patterns of their pupils. Another complaint about PSHE was that in the 1998 version, PSHE, known then as PSD (Personal and Social Development), was sub-divided into three strands, namely, Interacting and Working with others, Independent and Organisational Skills, and Attention. The splitting of PSD into strands allowed teachers to describe their pupils in a more nuanced way thereby providing more information about the pupils' development.

There has been no response to this complaint by the DCSF, and the result is that there are still a few teachers who want to know how to assess their pupils who are working above P8 in PSHE. Despite this, the maximum score allowed for PSHE remains at P8 and PSHE is still in one strand.

Comparison of the P scales with Alternative Assessment Schemes

The P scales are essentially level descriptions with each level containing a number of elements. They are intended as a framework to help teachers make best fit judgements that would place a student's performance at the appropriate P level taking into account the teacher's knowledge of individual pupils and the context in which the judgement is being made. Because the description of each level consists of elements it is possible to view a pupil's progress through levels as well as their progress within individual levels. While the progress through the levels can be seen as vertical progression the progress within levels can be viewed as lateral progression; it describes the expanse of a pupil's learning. The existence of elements within each level has led some professionals to develop alternative assessment systems by splitting the elements of the level descriptors of the P scales into sub-levels.

The alternative schemes, all originating from the P scales, are (1) Equals (2) PIVATS, (3) B-squared (4) Green Box and (5) CASPA.

Equals

Equals is a national organisation for teachers of pupils with learning difficulties. As an organisation, Equals is committed to improving the lives of children and young people with learning difficulties and disabilities through supporting high quality education. They have produced an assessment tool in the form of a document called The P scales Assessment of the National Curriculum from Equals (PACE) with which teachers can set improvement targets for their pupils. The Equals target setting document (PACE) was written to bring up to date, and in line with the new P scales, the original Baseline Assessment document produced by Equals in 1998 and accredited as a Baseline Assessment Scheme by QCA in September 1999. The PACE document was based on the P scales assessment criteria with each P level descriptor in PACE relating directly to the corresponding P level in the P scales. The current version of the Equals Assessment document is PACE2 which was written in order to accommodate the changes that arose as a result of the revision of the P scales in 2004. The difference between the P scales and Equals schemes is that whilst assessment of pupils' work using the P scales criteria is carried out by teachers using the best-fit approach, assessment of pupils using the Equals target setting document is based on pupils accomplishing the set tasks described for each P level. Each P level in the PACE document has an assessment activity directly linked to it. Although assessment activities are provided in the PACE document teachers are still expected to use their professional judgement to decide at which P level to assess a pupil. PACE aims to be more objective than the P scales proper because it involves the completion of tasks by pupils. There is some evidence to support the effectiveness of this approach. Whilst the correlations between the subject areas are high in the P scales data they are lower in the Equals data, indicating that whilst all the cognitive scales of the P scales measure the same construct, those of Equals measure more than one construct.

The Equals data collection project
Since 1999 the CEM at Durham University has collaborated with Equals in collating and analysing data collected by schools using the PACE target setting document. In the project, data are collected and analysed during the last term of the academic year, and the feedback processed and sent to schools before they complete the academic year in July. Two sets of feedback are sent to schools, the initial feedback and the value-added feedback. The initial feedback enables schools to compare the attainment levels of each pupil with those of other pupils of similar age in the sample. The value-added feedback contains the value added scores as well as predicted scores for the coming year. Therefore, apart from measuring the progress of each child using the value added, schools can also examine the predicted scores for each pupil.

Some teachers are critical of the Equals feedback from the data collection exercise. They think that grouping pupils of varying special needs in the feedback denies them the opportunity to compare the attainments and progress of pupils with same Special Educational Need. Some schools are also unhappy that the Equals data collection project excludes pupils whose attainment levels are above Level 2a of the National Curriculum.

More information about Equals can be found at http://www.equals.co.uk.

PIVATS

The Performance Indicators for Value-Added Target Setting (PIVATS) is for pupils who work below Level 1 of the National Curriculum. PIVATS was developed by Lancashire Local Authority and was based on the P scales level descriptors. The developers of PIVATS reasoned that it was too hard for pupils to achieve all the elements in a P scales level descriptor. Therefore they differentiated each of the P scales level descriptors from P1(i) to P8 and L1C to L4 of the National Curriculum into five steps. The idea was to make the levels more sensitive to pupils' efforts so that any progress no matter how small could be detected and recorded. In PIVATS all subject strands in the cognitive scales have levels P1(i) to P8 and National Curriculum L1c to 4.

In similarity with the P scales, PIVATS was designed to be used in making summative assessments for pupils working below National Curriculum Level 1 and was based on best-fit judgements. It could also be used in obtaining the baseline assessment of pupils at enrolment.

There are several differences in structure between the P scales assessment criteria and the PIVATS criteria.

- The P scales have five strands in their English Language subject area. There are four strands in PIVATS. In the P scales, English has only one strand for *Speaking and listening*. There are two strands of *Speaking and listening* in PIVATS with one strand named *Speaking and listening-comprehension* and the other named *Speaking and listening-expression*. There are as many strands of Mathematics and Science in PIVATS as there are in the P scales.
- There is only one strand of PSHE in the P scales with levels P1(i) to P8. On the other hand, PIVATS retains the three strands of Personal and Social Development found in the 1998 version of P scales. The strands are Interaction and working with others, Independent and Organisational skills, and Attention. Each of these three strands has 16 levels.

Lancashire LA also runs a PIVATS data collection and analysis service and processes feedback for schools. It is available on the web. As soon as schools enter their pupils' data they can access several items of the feedback such as individual pupil profiles, individual pupil performance tables, pupil summaries, audit trails and percentage movement in PIVATS.

More information about PIVATS can be found at http://www.lancashire.gov.uk/education/pivats/what_is_pivats/index.asp

B Squared

B Squared is another alternative assessment system for pupils working below Level 1 of the National Curriculum. The B Squared assessments come in packages, namely, P Steps and Small Steps, and can be used in assessing pupils in English, Mathematics and Science. P Steps assesses pupils from P1(i) to P8 while Small Steps covers Level 1 to Level 5 of the National Curriculum. There is also the Early Steps assessment designed for pupils under the age of 5 which covers the Foundation curriculum. These packages are available in hard copy and software versions.

In B Squared the curriculum is broken down, so that the focus is on individual targets instead of levels. Focusing on individual targets is intended to show teachers the pupil's progression through the level. It also helps parents to recognise the progress their children have made which could not have been possible if the focus was on the level as a whole.

Like the P scales, Equals and PIVATS, B Squared was designed to be used in summative assessment. However, they can be used as formative assessments when the resulting data are used to inform planning and target setting.

In place of the data collection and analysis projects of P scales, Equals and PIVATS, B Squared has a pupil tracking software known as Connecting Steps. The software allows the monitoring and analysis of whole school performance for the National Curriculum, P levels, the Foundation Curriculum and the Birth to Three Matters Curriculum. The software can also produce some reports for individual pupils for use in annual review processes.

More information about B Squared can be found at http://www.bsquared.co.uk/

Green Box

The Green Box is a software-based system developed by Andrew Martin, a former deputy head teacher of Greenside School in Stevenage. Essentially, it is a suite of ICT applications designed to store, maintain and present pupil assessment and progress information.

Green Box has four distinct parts, namely, Assessment pack, Target setting pack, IEP pack, and Achievement pack.

The assessment pack is designed to use P scales and National Curriculum descriptors in assessing pupils from P1(i) to Level 3 of the National Curriculum. It works by separating the individual statements of the P scales level descriptors and assesses each child according to how often they have performed each individual statement in the level. For each individual statement a pupil is scored one of the following:

0 for Never
1 for occasionally
2 for frequently
3 for consistently.

If a child demonstrates a statement frequently the number 2 will be selected against that statement. If the child never demonstrates the said statement 0 will be selected against the statement for that child.

The target setting function enables targets to be set and monitored. This is achieved using a spreadsheet in which each field represents a P-level statement. Names are entered on the assessment spreadsheet and the appropriate assessment value (0,1,2,3) is entered in each cell for the pupils and the cell coloured blue if the number on the cell is a target or green if the value is a target that has been achieved.

The Individual Education Plan (IEP) function tracks the IEP of each child over time.

The Achievement pack stores evidence of achievement in the form of digital photographs and video clips.

More information about Green Box is available at http://www.greenboxeducation.com

CASPA

CASPA (Comparison and Analysis of Special Pupil Attainment) was developed by SGA Systems Limited and described as a simple and easy-to-use tool to assist with the analysis and evaluation of attainment and progress of pupils with special educational needs. Like Equals, B Squared, PIVATS and Green Box it is based on the P scales and takes the form of software on which data is entered and analysis conducted.

Each of the assessment systems described here, P scales, Equals, PIVATS, B Squared, Green Box and CASPA can be used in the assessment of pupils working below Level 1 of the National Curriculum. However, while the P scales and Equals focus on the levels attained by the pupils, PIVATS, B Squared and Green Box focus on the sub-levels as they aim to be more sensitive to pupils' efforts. It is therefore at least theoretically possible with PIVATS,

B Squared and Green Box to explore further a pupil's attainment and progress.

Because PIVATS, B Squared and Green Box are all derived from the P scales, the question arises as to how appropriately a system like PIVATS links the sub-levels it has derived from P scales elements to the P scale levels. For example, how did PIVATS arrive at a conclusion that an element or statement within a P level, say, P4 of 'Writing', is equivalent to P4a, whilst another item or statement in the P4 description is equivalent to P4c. In other words, how was it established that the statement credited with P4a is more difficult to accomplish than the P4c statement; is P4a higher than P4c? Are there standard rules for allocating sub-levels to the items/statements within a level? This issue raises questions about the reliability of the sub-levels in PIVATS. The same applies to B Squared and Green Box.

Comparison of Objective Measures with Teacher Ratings

An objective measurement is one that depends on a measuring instrument which functions independently of the person doing the assessment. A measuring procedure would be considered objective if there is agreement (within an acceptable range of error) between measurements taken by two or more persons when they follow the same prescribed procedure. Hence, if a given number of persons were to score a test independently, they would obtain the same score for each pupil.

On the other hand tests or scoring systems would be considered subjective if two or more persons obtain scores that vary significantly when they test the same pupil.

Objective measurement systems need to access a concrete feature of the construct being measured. They also need to take subjectivity out of the assessment. Consider as an example, a teacher who wants to measure the *creative ability* of her students. Her first task would be to define what constitutes creative ability, and, assuming she accepts that '*ability to supply original responses to questions*' is the working definition of creative ability, then she will go ahead to design a test that will require her students to give responses which she will examine for originality. In this example, the operational definition of creative ability, namely, 'ability to supply original responses to questions', measures the construct and the concrete feature is the response of the student. The assessment might give a mark for each distinctly different idea in the response. This still leaves some judgement in the hands of the teacher, although this is kept to a minimum.

Non-objective measurement systems result in subjective judgements. For example, the grading of essay-like answers is mainly subjective. Several different examiners, though equally competent, will score the same essay differently because the perception of a written work varies from one person to the other and may even vary from day to day for the same person.

The P scales would be considered an objective assessment system if a child scored, say, P6 in 'Reading' no matter whether they were assessed by teacher A or teacher B. Therefore, the aim of designing an objective measuring system is to produce a system that can be used as a standard for measuring a construct.

In practice, assessments are often neither purely subjective nor purely objective but are rather a hybrid and exist somewhere on the continuum between the two.

In the light of the above definition it is clear that the P scales are a hybrid assessment. The P scales are not purely objective because assessment is based on a best-fit judgement and in many instances different teachers have awarded different P levels to same pupils. Because PIVATS, B Squared and Green Box are all derived from the P scales and, like the P scales, are based on teacher judgement, they are also hybrids. Although Equals is also derived from the P scales, assessment is not based entirely on teacher judgement because there are tasks that pupils must perform to score any particular P level; hence the data collected using the Equals assessment system exhibits the characteristics of objective measurement. As noted earlier in a comparative study of objective and self-report, that is, best-fit or

Pure subjectivity   Pure objectivity

Figure 7.1: The assessment continuum.

subjective performance measures, it was found that each assessment method appeared to measure a different aspect of the work, although each method was thought to be necessary.

Objective and subjective assessment systems can be compared by examining the correlation between the subjects in the data collected using the two systems. The correlation matrix for the P scales is shown in Table 7.1.

The very high correlations in Table 7.1 are typical of correlations when non-objective measures such as best-fit judgements have been used in assessments.

The very high correlations that exist between the Science strands ('Scientific enquiry', 'Life processes', 'Materials and their properties', 'Physical processes') and 'Writing' indicate that it is possible to predict Science scores using the scores in 'Writing'. This also implies that Science and 'Writing' measure the same construct. A similar comparison can be made between the Science strands and the Mathematics strands ('Using and applying', 'Number' and 'Shapes, space and measures') where the correlations are equally high.

Merits and Demerits of Objective Measures and Teacher Ratings

An objective measure is obtained by measuring something with a tight operationalisation of the construct. The factor being measured is tangible or is capable of being grasped fairly accurately. Therefore, objective measures are very reliable. On the other hand, a teacher rating depends on judgement, and because it depends on each individual teacher's judgement it varies from one teacher to another. Therefore teacher ratings have an inevitable degree of unreliability.

Many pupils in special schools, because of the nature of their Special Educational Needs, might be unable to respond to or participate in the activities involved in objective measurements; only teacher ratings will be applicable to such pupils. There are some activities that do not lend themselves to objective measurement. Teacher ratings are also appropriate to those parts of the curriculum.

Table 7.1: Table of correlations between subjects in the P scales 2007 data and based on 25,242 pupils

	Speak.	Listen.	Read	Write.	Using	Numb.	Shapes	Sci. enq.	Life proc.	Mat. & prop.
Speaking										
Listening	0.94									
Reading	0.84	0.86								
Writing	0.82	0.83	0.91							
Using	0.85	0.86	0.87	0.87						
Number	0.84	0.85	0.89	0.89	0.93					
Shapes	0.86	0.86	0.88	0.87	0.94	0.93				
Sci. enq.	0.82	0.82	0.80	0.80	0.85	0.83	0.85			
Life proc.	0.81	0.81	0.80	0.80	0.85	0.84	0.85	0.98		
Mat. & prop.	0.82	0.82	0.80	0.80	0.85	0.84	0.86	0.98	0.98	
Phys.proc.	0.82	0.82	0.80	0.80	0.84	0.83	0.85	0.97	0.98	0.98

Problems and the implications of P Scale use

From September 2008 the use of P scales for children with Special Educational Needs who are working below Level 1 of the National Curriculum will become statutory according to the Department for Children, Schools and Families (DCSF) and the Qualifications and Curriculum Authority (QCA). Schools will need to use the P scales to record and report the achievements and progress of those children in the core subjects of English, Mathematics and Science. This applies to both special and mainstream schools.

We can expect that a few problems will arise from making the use of the P scales statutory if all schools are using the scales as published by the DCSF/QCA. Problems will arise if a number of schools are using versions of the P scales that are, though derived from the DCSF/QCA version, different from it. These versions include PIVATS, B Squared and Green Box in which the levels have been split into several sub-levels in one way or another. It will become difficult if not impossible to compare the attainments and progress of all pupils.

Another source of worry in making the P scales statutory is the non-existence of a standard procedure of applying the best-fit judgement to pupils' work. A standard procedure should be established so that assessment procedures will be uniform.

Perhaps the greatest danger, however, is that the data will be made publicly available and converted into league tables. This would have serious consequences for the validity of the P scales data as the professionalism of teachers would be severely strained.

The Way Forward

The way forward must be the development of a system or the adoption of an existing system that will accommodate all schools and pupils for whom the National Curriculum does not apply. There must be only one assessment system to which all schools will subscribe so that valid comparisons between pupils and between schools can be made as required. The system developed or adopted must have standard methods of application. This would eliminate the inconsistencies that currently occur in assessments using the P scales and other alternative systems.

Further Reading

Brown FG (1983) *Principles of Educational and Psychological Testing*, 3rd edn. New York: Holt, Rinehart and Winston.

Pransky G, Finklestein S, Berndt E, Kyle M, Mackell J and Tortorice D (2006) Objective and self-report work performance measures: a comparative analysis, *International Journal of Productivity and Performance Management*, 55(2), 390–399.

Index

Note: Page numbers in *italics* refer to Figures, those in **bold** to Tables.